I LIKE BIG BOOKS AND I CANNOT LIE

a different sort of handbook for readers

by

LORI OSTER

ECKHARTZ
PRESS

For Sir Mix-A-Lot, who shared his fondness of ample derrières with the world.

TABLE OF CONTENTS

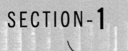

INTRODUCTION

1
2
3
4
5
6
7
8

Return This Book

If you have any desire at all to read a book of your own choosing, for heaven's sake put this handbook down and start reading that book.

If you are looking to improve your reading skills because you enjoy reading and you have the time to read books that interest you, put this handbook down and go read those books.

You see, the best way to improve your reading skills is to read because you want to.

If, on the other hand, you find yourself in a situation where you need to become a better reader and you need to do it now, stick with me. Or worse, if you have no desire to read at all, but you are in a situation where you must read to accomplish a greater goal, such as passing a class, or earning a diploma, or performing better at work, then this handbook is for you. In that case, let's get started, shall we?

Why Bother?

In my decade of working with students in reading courses I've heard it all: *reading is boring; I hate reading; I never read a book in high school, and I still graduated; reading is a waste of time.*

The thing is, all of these things are true. Sometimes.

Reading is boring. Reading can be boring, especially if it takes you a long time to read because you lack the skills to read faster.

I hate reading. Most people have been forced to read something they don't want to read, and it's easy to feel like you hate reading in this situation. I'm not particularly fond of reading long legal documents, for example, but fortunately I'm skilled enough that I can quickly scan things I don't want to read and locate the necessary information in a short amount of time.

I never read an entire book in high school, and I still graduated. Well, this isn't exactly something of which to be proud. If you made it through high school and never read a book, that condemns the current state of affairs in American public education rather than reading itself. Sadly, many educators are forced to prioritize standardized testing over more valuable activities like reading, artistic pursuits, or class discussions. This isn't the teachers' fault, by the way. But I digress.

If you made it through high school without reading a book, you probably developed some interesting compensatory skills to make up for your lack of reading. Those skills will serve you well if you put them to good use. More about that later.

Reading is a waste of time. Sure, this can be true. Reading is a colossal waste of time if you read without comprehending the text, or if you comprehend but forget everything you read the day after you read it. It's also a waste of time if you read without a purpose and therefore have no idea what to focus on and what to ignore.

You may think the reading you're required to do for a class is a waste of time, too, but I disagree. Are you taking this class because it's required to, say, earn a degree? Is earning this degree a goal of yours? If so, then the reading is a necessary step on your path to making one of your goals a reality. Doesn't sound like a waste of time to me.

The truth is: Reading puts you on the receiving end of great ideas. We live in a time and place with access to some of the greatest ideas ever written. All you need to do is pick them up, or look them up, and read them. And if you are a student, reading is your best tool for success. Most of the information we share in academia comes in written form. If you are unable or unwilling to read as skilled readers do, you are going to miss out on the very thing that makes a college education worth it: ideas.

Reading: Some Background Information

Reading is a Process

A process is *a series of action or steps taken to achieve an end.* In other words, a process involves several different actions in order to accomplish a goal. All too often, struggling readers think of reading as something that you either "get" or "don't get." I've had students tell me "I'm just a bad reader" or "I can't read."

Here's the thing: As a process, there are a lot of different steps involved with reading well, so it is nearly impossible for someone to just plain *be* a bad reader. The issue these students usually face is that they either never learned about some of the most important steps involved with reading, or they did learn about them and simply haven't practiced them enough. Which brings me to my next point . . .

It takes time and practice to become a skilled reader. People aren't good readers because they were naturally born good readers. They're good readers because they spent many years reading, and over time that experience has paid off. On the flip side, people aren't poor readers because they were naturally born poor readers. They're poor readers because they haven't read very much, or they have read but never made the effort to understand what they've read and over time haven't developed into expert readers.

Chances are, you're reading this book because you need some help becoming an expert reader. Here's the good news: Reading is not rocket science. Almost anyone who is eager to become a better reader *can* become a better reader. Are you ready for the bad news? Here it is: It's going to take a lot of time and practice. If you want to develop your reading skills you are going to have to commit to the following:

1. Read every day, ideally for at least one hour per day.
2. Apply the skills we discuss in this book to all of the reading you do.
3. Write every day, preferably in response to your reading.
4. Repeat.

There is no magic pill. You may be reading this book after years of *not practicing* skilled reading. Think of it this way: If you wanted to join a college basketball team, but you haven't been playing basketball for years, how much practice do you think it would take to become a college-level basketball player? Now, insert the word *reading* wherever you see the word *basketball,* and I think you'll get my drift.

What Does an Expert Reader Look Like?

Expert readers are everywhere—in offices, grocery stores, shopping centers, cars, and of course, in schools. Expert readers know how to read different types of writing for different purposes, and they know how to read them effectively.

Expert readers are equipped with a toolkit filled with strategies and skills that help them get the information they need from the various texts they read, and they often don't even realize they are using them. Once you develop the skills you need to be an expert reader, the process starts to feel automatic, just like any other skill you've mastered. Think about learning to drive a car—did it feel natural at first, or did you have to think about every little thing you needed to do in order to get the car from point A to point B? Now think about how much easier it is to get in your car and drive now that you have been doing it for a while. (If you don't drive, think about any other skill that you have learned and mastered. Maybe you are an excellent chef, painter, beat boxer, or snowboarder.)

Becoming an expert reader is just like becoming skilled at anything else. It takes time to learn all of the habits and skills you need in order to do it well, but once you've mastered it, reading will feel automatic and easy. That's a promise.

One More Thing about Reading

We read for many reasons, but I feel compelled to share that I believe the chief benefit of reading is that it encourages you to think for yourself, to develop original thought, and to transform in some way. In other words, reading is a vital endeavor for anyone who wants to live a fulfilled life, and my hope is that you will be able to get even one fraction of the joy out of reading that I experience, myself.

I read every day. I read a novel just for fun for at least an hour every night. I read the Sunday paper every week. I read research articles about education and literacy for work several times a week. And I read reviews of books nearly every day. And I enjoy it all.

Four Things to Know About Reading

The best way to become a better reader is to read.

There is no magic bullet, or strategy, or tip that I can give you to help you become a better reader. We can work on developing your comprehension skills, your fluency, your vocabulary, your retention of material read; but none of that work will mean anything if you don't put it to use and *read*.

Your reading ability varies based on what you're reading.

It's a common misconception today that students have "a reading level" that can be identified by taking a test or an informal reading inventory. These assessments are excellent ways to give students an idea of their reading ability, but the results will vary depending on several factors:

- Your interest in a text
- Your motivation for reading, and
- Your perception of how relevant the reading is to your life

This means that the more you are interested and motivated to read something, the easier it will be for you to understand, and thus, the higher you would score on a test based on that reading.

You need to find your reading zone.

My current reading zone involves an overstuffed sofa, a warm blanket, at least one cat or dog curled up next to me, and a table within reach that holds a mug of hot coffee, a pen, and my reading notebook. Most important of all is that my reading zone is *silent*. This is the environment in which I do my best reading, and this is *my* zone, so back off. You need to find your own zone.

Maybe you do your best reading in the local coffee shop by your house with your iPod and some hot cocoa, or in a study carrel at the library, or at your best friend's house with music blaring in the background. Whatever it includes and wherever it is, you need to find and claim your own reading zone. Think of it as just another tool for getting the most out of every reading.

There are five components to the reading process.

If you are reading this right now, you have already mastered the first and second components. (CONGRATULATIONS!) Therefore, we'll be focusing on the last three components in this book.

The five components of the reading process:
1. *Phonemic awareness*—The recognition that individual sounds create words.
2. *Phonics*—The knowledge of the relationships between written letters and spoken sounds.
3. *Fluency*—The ability to read at an appropriate rate with accuracy, expression, and phrasing
4. *Vocabulary*—The knowledge of words, their definitions, and usage.
5. *Comprehension*—The ability to understand, remember, and communicate what is read.

About the Reading Skills and My Particular Approach to Teaching Reading

I present the reading skills individually in this book because this is the easiest way for you to learn about them and to identify which skills you need to practice in order to become a better reader.

However, when reading we *rarely* apply one skill in isolation. (In fact, it is a bit inaccurate to call them *skills* at all. They are more accurately *ways of thinking*, but more on this later.) The act of reading involves the fluid integration of several different skills (or ways of thinking) all at once. It is important for you to remember this while using this book.

While it is helpful to initially practice using a new reading skill on its own, as soon as you are comfortable applying that skill you should incorporate it into your overall reading process moving forward.

Think of the way we teach new drivers how to operate a car:

First, we might teach a new driver how the different pedals work. Then, we may teach him how to use the steering wheel, and then the turn signals, how to operate the windows, etc. However, when we put him behind the wheel, we expect him to combine all of the things he's learned in order to drive the car in a safe and effective manner. We would never ask a new driver to *only* practice using the pedals while driving—that would be preposterous! He wouldn't get anywhere, would he? Reading works in a similar way. It is helpful to first focus on each skill individually, but readers won't get very far unless they practice applying all of their skills together.

In other words, the skills are important, but they are simply the best way I know to help you develop *behaviors* that will lead to comprehension, and it is *comprehension* that is our ultimate goal. Do not get caught up in the skills themselves; they are tools for helping you develop the ability to understand and use what you read.

How to Get the Most Out of this Book

This book can only give you information, it is up to you to develop new ways of thinking while reading. You will learn about the ways expert readers think while reading, which I will call reading skills for the sake of brevity—what they are, how to use them, and when. Learning *about* the skills, however, is the easy part.

The hard work comes in actually applying the skills. In practice. Every day. And this is where you come in. The truth is no book can make you a better reader. It is you who must do all the hard work and actually *practice* the skills on a regular basis as you develop new ways of thinking about reading.

It's likely that you are already quite good at applying some of these skills to reading. The key here is to figure out *which of these skills you already posses and which of these skills you need to develop.* You have likely developed several reading habits that have helped you get to where you are today. Some of these habits are good habits, and some of these may be bad habits. One thing that will make a tremendous difference in your growth as a reader will be self-reflection.

As you learn about each reading skill, ask yourself whether you have already developed the habit of applying that skill while reading. If you have, then you can skim that section and smile with the knowledge that you have already mastered a key ingredient of reading well. If you have not yet mastered the skill, take copious notes and begin practicing that skill immediately, every time you read.

It may take you a week, a month, or even years to master

a particular reading skill. Your growth will depend on your own commitment to applying the skills you need and whether you practice them regularly.

Recommended Approach

Practice reading regularly. At minimum, one hour daily if you're serious about becoming a better reader.

If you are not ready or willing to read at least every day, preferable for one hour a day, I strongly recommend you reconsider your reasons for reading this book. If you are reading this as a requirement for a course, odds are that you need to become a stronger reader to achieve your academic goals. The only way to accomplish this purpose is to read, regularly and over a long period of time. If this seems like more than you are currently willing to handle, think about why you are attending school in the first place, and I urge you to be honest with yourself about whether you are truly ready to get the most out of it.

Students who are enrolled in *at least* six hours of college-level courses or high school students with a regular class schedule will experience the greatest growth in their reading skills. This is because these students have a lot of opportunities for applying their newly learned reading skills to texts as they often have a lot of reading to do for their courses.

If you are reading this book and you are a college student who is not enrolled in at least two college-level courses, I strongly recommend that you reconsider your current class schedule or that you read *at least 50 pages* of material every week. It is unlikely that you will develop the reading skills you desire if you don't have regular opportunities to apply them to actual reading.

The biggest mistake you can make is to believe that you are

too good for this book. If you are a student, odds are you took a reading test, and your results on that test placed you into a required reading course. Your instructor will likely spend the first two weeks of the semester assessing your reading ability to make sure that you belong in the course. If he or she does not tell you that you should have been placed in a higher course, then you need this course and this book. Don't tell yourself otherwise. Use this time to develop the skills you need. Take advantage of your time in class. In my opinion, it will be one of the most valuable courses of your academic career.

Regardless of why you chose to pick up this book, everyone, no matter their skill level, can benefit from learning these principles and putting them into practice.

One More Time for Good Measure: It's Not Really About the "Skills", It's About Developing Ways of Thinking

The reading practices I discuss in this book are simple. A quick look at the Table of Contents might make someone think this book is too elementary to be of any use. However, if you want to become a better reader, it is not enough to *know* which skills make a good reader, you must develop new ways of thinking about the things you read. In other words, the work you have ahead of you is to transform your thought process while reading, a thing easier said than done. This book will help you do just that, step by step.

To illustrate this point, consider an example: If I want to get in better physical shape, I could eat fewer calories, eat healthy foods, and exercise regularly. It's easy to know what I need to do to, isn't it? But knowing that I should be eating better and moving more isn't enough to change my dress size. The difficult part is putting these things into action. The reading skills are no different. Think of them as habits, perhaps, rather than skills. And as I said earlier, practicing the skills is not even your ultimate goal. Your ultimate goal is to read with comprehension. The skills are the tools that will help you get there.

Now that we have all that out of the way, you're ready to get to work. Happy reading!

Are You "Getting" it?
The First Step to Changing Your Way of
Thinking: Self-Assessment & Reflection

Reading is a tricky skill to teach because the good stuff happens in your head while you read, and so all readers look similar to observers: head bent down, eyes scanning pages, book open, pages turning. We teachers have no way of discerning whether our students are actually focused on the text, let alone comprehending it. For all we know, they could be thinking about how much they really want some cheese fries. (I often say we should recruit mind readers to teach reading courses for this very reason, but for some reason this idea is consistently ignored.)

This is the reason reading teachers and reading textbooks ask you to answer questions about texts or write summaries after you read. Since we cannot read your mind, we have to ask you to *tell us* about what you read so we can then *tell you* how well you understood it and what you should do moving forward.

There is a major flaw in this approach because **it keeps learners (you) dependent on others (teachers, professors, textbook answer guides) for feedback about their reading ability.** This kind of dependence is fine for beginning readers, but if you're reading this book, you need more independence. You need to become capable of determining how well you understand a text without anyone else's help.

All of the skills in this book will teach you to do just that. Before we move on to the individual skills, I'm going to show you a quick and easy way to check if you "get" what you just read. This check will give you general feedback about whether you're on track, or whether you need to do some rereading before you move on.

Are you ready? Read on.

I present to you:
The DO I GET IT? APP

You were excited for a moment, weren't you? You thought I had a downloadable app that can read your mind and tell you whether you understand a reading. Sorry to disappoint, but as I shared earlier, you are going to have to put in more work than that to become a better reader.

The **Do I Get it? App** is an easy way to start gaining independence and monitoring your own reading comprehension.

Here's how the **DO I GET IT? APP** works:
Every time you finish reading something, and I mean *every time,* answer the following:

A: What was the reading ABOUT?
   You have one sentence to answer this. Give a general, overall description. If you can't do this, you probably didn't "get" it. If this is the case, it's time to reread. (Don't despair if you find yourself unable to do this first step; as you move through this book and work on the skills that follow, this step will become a piece of cake.) You should be able to complete this step in under one minute.

P: What was the POINT of the reading?
   In other words, why does the reading exist? What is the purpose of the reading? Common purposes are: to inform, to persuade, to entertain. If you can't figure it out, you probably didn't "get" it, and it's time to reread. You should be able to complete this step in under one minute.

P: Who or what are the main PLAYERS in the reading? By *players* I mean *main characters* (in fiction) and *main concepts or ideas* (in nonfiction). Take one minute to identify the major players in the reading. If you can't easily name them, you probably didn't "get" it, and you should probably reread the piece. You should be able to complete this step in less than one minute.

The **Do I Get it? App** is a quick (three minutes tops!) method to check yourself after reading something. My recommendation is to get into the habit of using the Do I Get it? App as soon as possible, which means *right now*. You *are* reading something right now, aren't you? Well, this is the perfect time to give the Do I Get it? App a try. When you finish reading this page ask yourself the three questions (About, Point, Players) and see how well you "got" what you just read.

Next Steps: Start using the **Do I Get it? App** every time you read. It will help you become an independent, self-reflective reader, which is, after all, the reason you're reading this book, right?

Timeout For Self-Assessment

Now that you've read this very long introduction to reading, *(you did read it, didn't you? If not, I implore you to stop reading this page and go back right now. This stuff is important!)* and now that you have the **Do I Get it? App** down, it's time to take a step back and assess your current habits and reading ability.

Take some time to write down the following information. Keep this information somewhere accessible so you'll be able to find it and marvel at your progress later on.

- The next three or four things you read, note how long it takes you to read them. Then, record the # of pages and your reading time.
- How often do you read something and realize that you don't remember what you just read when you get to the end? Does this happen more often with certain types of readings?
- What do you do when you find an unfamiliar word in the reading? Do you skip it? Look up the definition? Highlight it? Try to figure out its meaning on your own?
- Do you read *every word* in a text, or do you skip words, sentences, or paragraphs?
- If you are reading something that contains charts, pictures, or other special features, do you read them or skip over them?
- What comes to mind when you hear the word *reading?* Be honest!
- In what environment do you read? Is there noise in the background, such as music, television, or other people? Do you have your phone or a computer nearby while

you read? Where are you sitting when you read? How is the light?

- How often do you find yourself distracted from a reading? Do you check text messages or Facebook while reading? Do you stop to grab a snack? Do you divide your time between the reading and any other things?
- If you are a student, how well do you do on assignments or tests based on readings? Do you do poorly even though you read the assigned readings?
- If you are a student, when do you do your assigned readings for class? Do you rush to read them at the last minute, or do you start them early enough so you won't have to rush?

If you are looking at this long list and starting to wonder whether this is going to be worth the effort, trust me, it is. If you're reading this book it's fair to guess that you have found yourself frustrated with your reading ability at some point, and perhaps your reading ability is holding you back from achieving an important goal.

The things I am going to ask you to do in this book may seem time-consuming in the moment, but in the long run they will *save you time* by helping you become the expert reader that you can and should be. I often tell my students that reading without comprehension is like running on a treadmill without burning calories. This book will help you stop wasting your time on the frustrated reader treadmill.

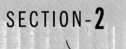

SECTION-2

READING COMPREHENSION

Remember: Comprehension is the ability to understand, remember, and communicate what you read. In order to improve your reading comprehension, we are going to discuss the habits that good readers employ before, during, and after reading, and how to apply them.

Before Reading Skills

Activate Prior Knowledge
Preview
Set a Purpose
Predict
Connect
Question

During Reading Skills

Metacognition
Identify Topic & Main Idea
Identify Text Structures
Identify Text Features
Predict Outcomes
Annotate

During & After Reading Skills

Read Critically: Distinguish between Fact and Opinion
Read Critically: Identify Author's Purpose
Read Critically: Recognize Generalizations
Read Critically: Identify Bias
Read Critically: Identify Tone
Read Critically: Recognize Validity

After Reading Skills
Retell
Reread
Make Judgments and Draw Conclusions
Infer
Identify Use of Imagery and Figurative Language
Respond

This list is by no means exhaustive. Rather, these are the skills that have been the most helpful for my students over the years.

Before Reading:
ACTIVATE PRIOR KNOWLEDGE

The prior knowledge you bring to a reading is a combination of what you **know,** what you **believe,** and what you've **experienced.**

What you know: This includes your knowledge of the topic, the author, of the main idea, and even what you know about reading and the type of writing you're about to read.

What you believe: This includes your beliefs about yourself as a reader, your motivation and desire to read, and your beliefs about the ideas expressed in the reading.

What you've experienced: This includes your experiences that relate to the reading, to details within the reading, and the experiences you've had with reading in general.

Why is prior knowledge so important (and powerful) for readers?

Prior knowledge is powerful because the only way you learn new information is by connecting it to existing information. This point is so important that I'm going to do something I don't often do; I'm going to repeat myself:

Learning happens when you connect new information to existing information.

This means that if you'd like to learn something new, you *must* connect the new information you're taking in to existing information you already have. The existing information you already have? That is what we call prior knowledge.

This is all nice to know, but let's get down to brass tacks:

How do skilled readers activate their prior knowledge before reading?

Skilled readers ask and answer some questions *before* reading, such as:

- What do I know about this topic or style of writing?
- What do I know about this author?
- What experiences have I had that relate to this?
- What have I read before that relates to this?
- What do I think about this topic or style of writing?
- What do I think about this author?
- What personal experiences or ideas does this topic remind me of?

This seems like a lot of work—what benefits do readers get out of this?

This may seem like a lot of work at first, but remember—all of these skills become automatic with practice and experience. Just as skilled drivers automatically put the key in the ignition, fasten the seatbelt, adjust the rear view mirror, turn on the heat or a/c, and adjust the radio as soon as they get into the car, skilled readers go through a series of thinking before they even begin reading. You will too, once you've practiced these skills long enough. That's a promise.

To answer the question, activating prior knowledge has many benefits for readers.

- Activating prior knowledge:
- Increases comprehension
- Increases fluency (so you can read faster with more accuracy)
- Makes the reading personally relevant, and therefore, it also:
  - Increases motivation to read (you're more motivated to read something if you can personally relate to it. We'll talk more about this later on.)

In other words, **activating prior knowledge saves time and frustration**. Just as people don't want to bother running on a treadmill if they aren't going to burn calories, nobody wants to read if they aren't going to understand and remember what they read. Activating prior knowledge is one step toward ensuring that readers benefit from the time they spend reading.

By the way—all of the strategies we are going to discuss in this book have similar benefits to activating prior knowledge. Remember that!

Actions speak louder than words:

What do readers look like while Activating Prior Knowledge?

Readers probably look like they're sitting around and wasting time when they're activating prior knowledge. Some might squint their eyes and hold their chin in one hand in a pensive posture. Others might have their mouths hanging open and a glazed look in their eyes. But in their heads they're all *thinking*. And that, my friends, is the key.

Next Steps

The next time you sit down to read something be sure to activate your prior knowledge *before you read*.

Step 1. Look at the title, the author, any graphics or pictures in the reading, and skim the text. If you're reading for a class, think about the lecture or lesson that was given to lead up to this reading. In other words, size up the text before you read it. Get a feel for what it is about.

Step 2. Ask yourself what you know, believe, and have experienced related to the reading. See the questions on the previous page if you've forgotten the questions to ask yourself.

Step 3. Answer the questions you just asked yourself! This is the step that many people skip over, yet it is the most important step to take.

Step 4. At this point, you should feel like you've flooded your brain with ideas, thoughts, feelings, and memories related to the text you're about to read. *This is the point of activating your prior knowledge, by the way.* If you don't feel the flood, that's okay, but it probably means you simply don't have enough prior knowledge about the subject to get yourself sufficiently prepared. If this is the case, then it's time to consult the Internet—do a quick Google search for the subject, get some background information, and then return to Step 1.

Step 5. Now you're ready to read. Go ahead and read the text, and while reading keep in mind all of the prior knowledge you just pulled into the forefront of your thoughts. You should experience increased comprehension while reading, and you should also remember the reading longer than if you hadn't activated your prior knowledge.

In addition to the above, reflect on the following after trying out this skill for a week or so:

- Now that you are activating your prior knowledge, do you notice a difference in your reading comprehension, or in the amount of information you can recall after reading?
  - If the answer is no and if you are still experiencing difficulty comprehending or remembering what you read, perhaps you need to get some of these thoughts out of your head and onto paper. Jot down your thoughts instead of just thinking them. It will be most helpful to write your ideas in the margins of the text or on sticky notes that you can place onto the reading itself.
  - If the answer is no but you are comprehending what you read just fine and don't need any help, then why are you still reading this book?
  - If the answer is yes, keep on doing what you're doing.
- Most expert readers automatically activate prior knowledge before reading without even recognizing that they are doing it. Pay attention to your pre-reading habits, and congratulate yourself when you realize that you are activating prior knowledge without having to remind yourself to do so. This is a big deal, as you are one step closer to becoming an expert reader. Well done!

Before Reading:
PREVIEW

Why is previewing so important (and powerful) for readers?

Previewing helps you get a feel for the reading before you dive into actually reading it. Depending on the type of reading you're doing, previewing will help you familiarize yourself with the writing style, the organization, or the content of the text. In other words, previewing helps *set the mood* for your reading—it prepares you to really get into whatever it is you're about to read.

Think about movie previews, what do they normally include? The highlights of the movie, right? The most exciting action scene, the moment two characters are about to kiss, or the funniest lines that will get the biggest laughs. Movie previews are designed to get audiences interested in a movie so they'll spend a whopping $10 for the privilege of watching it. But they have another function: they help audiences follow the story better. Have you ever watched a movie after seeing a preview for it and known that a great line was coming up? Or you knew that two characters would end up together before they even looked at each other on screen? That's the power of previewing.

This is all nice to know, but let's cut to the chase:

How do readers preview before reading?

First, look at the following (if they exist) **before** you read:

1. The title and author
2. Images—graphs, pictures, charts, etc.
3. Text on the cover and back cover of the piece
4. The introductory paragraph/s
5. Headings and subheadings
6. Unique text that is *italicized*, bolded, colored, highlighted, CAPITALIZED, underlined, listed, written in the margins, and any other text that stands out.

Second, take some time to consider each of the items listed above, and ask yourself:

1. What do I think this reading is about?
2. If you're reading for a class: What does my teacher or professor want me to get out of this reading?

Third, set some expectations for the reading based on what you've just found.

1. Do you have any **prior knowledge** about this material? (This **prior knowledge** concept should sound familiar to you. If not, go back and read the previous section.)
2. Do you have any questions about the material?

3. Do you think you will need additional support to understand what you are about to read?
   - If the answer is *yes*, then go ahead and find that support. Reach out to your professor, perhaps, or your good friend, Google, and get some more background knowledge before you move forward.

Actions speak louder than words:

Just Do It:
What do readers look like while Previewing?

You can tell a reader is previewing material if she's flipping through pages and scanning the material. She might look like she's trying to find something specific, and she might pause every now and then after seeing something to activate some PK. (She'll do this last bit if she really wants to read the piece well.)

Next Steps

The next time you sit down to read something be sure to preview the reading *before you read.*

Step 1. Follow the steps listed above in *How Do Readers Preview Before Reading.*

Step 2. Pay attention to what you've found while following those steps. Jot your ideas down in the margins of the text or on sticky notes, and refer back to them as you read.

Step 3. Over time, reflect on whether previewing is helping you to comprehend and remember what you read. If you feel that it isn't helpful, then perhaps you aren't doing it thoroughly enough. Also make sure to note when it becomes automatic to you, and give yourself another pat on the back because that means you are becoming a stronger reader.

Before Reading:
SET A PURPOSE

Why is setting a purpose so important (and powerful) for readers?

Setting a purpose helps you focus on what is important, and therefore it helps you avoid information overload. Reading without a purpose can lead to confusion, frustration, and other negative things that are likely to discourage you from reading.

Over the years I've noticed that my students who are most frustrated with reading often find that this one skill alone changes the entire game for them. Perhaps this can be true for you, too.

In addition, setting a purpose:
- Encourages you to read *actively*
- Helps you activate your *background knowledge* (which, as you already know, is an extremely important skill)
- Helps you *self-assess* whether you are comprehending the reading
- Makes it easier to *locate the information* that is important to you (and ignore the information that isn't!)

This is all nice to know, but let's get down to brass tacks:

How do readers set a purpose for themselves before reading?

First, consider your purpose for reading. Or, if you're reading for class, consider whether your instructor has a specific purpose in mind for the reading.

1. How has your instructor expected you to apply the information from readings in the past—to support a class discussion? To answer specific questions? To take a quiz or test? To engage in an activity, such as a lab or group project?
2. If you know how your instructor plans to use the reading in class, keep this in mind when you consider the next step, and set a purpose that will help you in class.

Second, set a purpose for reading. Here are some examples: Ask questions. Plan to ask questions about the text as you read.

1. Create discussion questions. Plan to imagine yourself leading a discussion about the text and create questions that you could ask your peers.
2. Make connections. Plan to make connections to the characters, events, information, or anything else you read about in the text. (More on this later.)
3. Make predictions. Plan to make predictions about what will happen next in the story, or about what you will learn about next while reading.
4. Agree or disagree. Plan to have a conversation with the author while reading, and plan to note when you agree or disagree with the author's assertions.
5. Identify the main idea. This one is a throwback to your good old junior high days, I'm sure, but there's a reason we teach students to identify the main idea. It's an important key for understanding what you read. Tell yourself you will identify the main idea while reading, and then do it.
6. Make an inference. Plan to take the information you read and draw conclusions based on it before you reach the end of the text.

7. Retell. Plan to pause after reading and do a quick retell of what you just read. (This is a powerful study tool that we will discuss later in the book.)

8. Visualize a picture. Plan to visualize the details of the text in your mind. This works very well with many complex concepts that you'll find yourself learning about in math and science courses, especially.

9. Identify author bias. Plan to identify author bias if it exists, and it can (and often does) exist in almost any text you read, including a textbook.

Third, set clear and measurable goals:

1. How many annotations do you plan to make?
   a. An annotation is a marking you make in the text while reading. (You can make these marks in your notebook or on a sticky note if you prefer, but I believe that marking up the text itself is the most helpful because it places your thoughts about the text exactly where and when you have them while reading.) Before you start reading, give yourself a goal to make a certain amount of marks in the text, e.g. "I will make at least eight annotations while reading." This is important to help keep yourself engaged in the reading.

2. How much do you plan to read ~or~ for how long do you plan to read? Your goal must be clear and measurable, meaning that you will know without a doubt whether you achieve your goal or not. e.g. "I will create four discussion questions in the next 20 minutes," or "I will make two connections and two predictions in the next 15 pages."

This final step is extremely important, as it helps you keep yourself engaged in the reading, and if your mind does drift

off while reading, it helps you get yourself back on track or
gives you a reason to get back on track.

Actions speak louder than words:

Just Do It: What do readers look like while Setting a Purpose?

Readers who are setting a purpose for their reading will be
jotting down some notes in the margins of their text or in
their notebook to help them remember their purpose.

They may also be talking to classmates or their instructor
to get some more information about what their purpose
should be. Smart students do this when they aren't exactly
sure about their purpose for reading, and they don't want to
waste any time reading for the wrong purpose, so they get the
information up front.

Next Steps

The next time you sit down to read something, set a purpose
for your reading by following the steps outlined above. As
you do this, be sure to reflect on whether you are fulfilling
the purpose you set for yourself, and whether doing so helps
you read with more comprehension and recall. If you find
that this skill is not helping you, then perhaps you still need
to work on it a bit. As with activating prior knowledge and
previewing, setting a purpose will become a habit over time.

If you find yourself struggling with this one, an easy way
to help yourself set and fulfill your purpose is to write it at
the top of the reading. Writing things down, as you'll see,
is a powerful tool for helping yourself to focus and follow
through on things while reading.

Before Reading:
PREDICT

Why predicting so important (and powerful) for readers?

A prediction is an educated guess about what you are about to read. Predicting is another way to prepare yourself for reading because it gets you involved with the text before you even read it. Predicting comes after you've already activated your prior knowledge, set a purpose for reading, and previewed, so it is one more step in anticipating the reading before you actually read it.

Predictions are powerful tools for readers. Not only do they help you stay focused on the reading by giving you a specific purpose, but they help you become interested in the reading. When you're forced to read something, the chances are pretty high that you won't have much interest in it.

However, you can use predictions to make a game out of the reading: If you make two correct predictions, reward yourself with a small break or a snack. The reward doesn't have to be large, and it might seem cheesy right now, but sometimes a small treat is all it takes to transform your reading experience from a chore to something you actually want to complete. I prefer Cheez-Its or popcorn, myself.

The power of prediction goes beyond just piquing the reader's interest: Predictions help you identify important information, and even better, *retain* important information. The simple act of making a prediction causes your brain to focus on the outcome in a way that it wouldn't otherwise do. Think about this: If a psychic told you that you were going to meet a tall, dark-haired stranger who would become the love of your life, wouldn't you start paying more attention to the brunettes walking around? I bet you would.

This is all nice to know, but let's get down to brass tacks:

How do readers predict before reading?

First, consider your prior knowledge about the subject, your purpose for reading, and the information you acquired when you previewed the material. Let these things guide the type of predictions you make.

Second, make predictions based on what you've already discovered about the reading:

- Will you enjoy reading this text?
- Will you agree with the author?
- What is the main idea?
- Is this author biased?
- Which concepts will be explained next in the text?
- How will this text compare to other information you've read about the subject?
- How will your instructor expect you to apply this information in class?

Actions speak louder than words:

Just Do It:
What do readers look like while Predicting?

Readers who are making predictions will usually wave their hands around a crystal ball. Some close their eyes and murmur words in strange languages as well.

I was just making sure you're still with me.

Readers who are making predictions are likely to jot notes down in the margins of the text or in their notebooks. They may flip ahead to get some clues if they're really desperate. If they're good at predicting, they'll take small breaks and eat snacks as a reward for correct predictions.

Next Steps

If you've been paying close attention thus far, you should have noticed a couple of things:

1. Several of these *before reading skills* seem to overlap. Prior knowledge supports previewing, and setting a purpose requires you to activate your prior knowledge and to preview, anyway. And in order to predict anything you'll have to preview first, right? Right.
2. Remember back in the introduction when I discussed my particular approach to teaching the reading skills? Well, just in case you forgot the details, I mentioned that even though I break each skill down and discuss it individually, reading actually requires the fluid integration of multiple skills at once. This is why there is so much overlap across the skills, because they don't really exist in isolation, and you can't really apply only one at a time while reading.

3. In the **Next Steps** section of each skill I remind you to pay attention to whether or not the skill is helping you read with more comprehension and recall. This reminder is designed to help you reflect on your growth as a reader and to identify which skills are helping you improve. This habit of reflection is vital for anyone who wishes to develop any skill, so I'm going to continue to remind you to reflect as you move through this book.

4. As for predicting, pay attention to whether your predictions are helping you read better, and by better I mean with more comprehension and the ability to remember what you read after you've read it. If, while reading, you find yourself thinking, *I totally knew that was going to be in here!*, that's a good sign that you are using the power of predictions correctly. If, on the other hand, you make predictions before reading and never revisit them while reading, you are not using the power of predictions to your advantage.

Before Reading:
CONNECT

Why is connecting so important (and powerful) for readers?

Connecting to the reading is so important because (as you already know from our little lesson on *prior knowledge)* learning happens when you connect new information to existing information.

I know what you're probably thinking: "Didn't I already do this when I activated my prior knowledge?" That's a really good thought, and yes, you did. However, this step is *so important,* that the reading brain has developed multiple methods of connecting new information to existing information, so we now have another skill to add to our reading toolkit: connecting.

In addition, making connections to the reading makes it more personally relevant to you, *and,* it makes it more familiar. Both of these things will make it easier for you to comprehend, retain, and apply the information you read. And, as a bonus, psychology tells us that we are more likely to remember things to which we make personal connections. This means connecting will not only help you comprehend, it will help you recall the information, too.

You can use connecting to your benefit outside of reading, as well. If you make connections with other students in your classes or, even better, with your instructors, you will find yourself more comfortable with the course and the course material. In other words, make friends with your classmates and use your instructors' office hours to get to know them.

This is all nice to know, but let's get down to brass tacks:

How do readers make connections before reading?

First, how can you personally connect to this reading?

- Do you have any personal experience with this subject?
- Do you have any personal experience with something related to this subject?
- Did anything look familiar to you while you were previewing?

Second, can anyone you know connect to this reading?

- Did your great aunt Martha once date a man who had an uncle who told stories about this subject? Voila! A connection.

Third, have you previously learned anything that can connect to this reading?

- Did you once see a show on the Discovery channel about this topic?
- Have you ever read anything else by this author?
- Have you ever heard/seen/read or experienced *anything* related to this topic?

Any connection you can make to the reading, no matter how trivial, will help. Trust me.

Actions speak louder than words:

Just Do It:
What do readers look like while Connecting?

Readers who are connecting will look a lot like the loafers we see doing any other pre-reading skill. They'll be staring at the sky, maybe even looking at things around them to see what they can connect to in their physical world.

Next Steps

I'm hoping by now you've already made some predictions about what the Next Steps will be based on what you've learned in the previous reading skills. If you did predict what I'm about to say, well done! You are already using some great reading skills. If you didn't, take this as a reminder to start putting the skills you've already read about to good use. Remember, it's not enough to *know* how an expert reader thinks; you have to actually *think like an expert reader* if you hope to become one.

So, Next Steps for Connecting:

First, pay attention to whether or not you are actually connecting to readings before you read. *Second,* make a mental note when you find yourself making connections automatically. At that point you'll have yet another reading skill down. Nice work.

Before Reading:
QUESTION

Why is questioning so important (and powerful) for readers?

Questioning is the last *before reading* skill we'll discuss, and it is important because it helps guide you as you dive into the actual reading by giving you a specific *focus*.

In addition, questioning:
- Encourages you to read *actively*
- Helps you identify information that is *personally meaningful* in the reading
- Helps you *self-assess* what you need to get out of the reading

This is all nice to know, but let's get down to brass tacks:

How do readers ask questions before reading?
First, consider the following:
- What do *I want* to know about this subject?
- What does *my professor want* me to know about this subject?
- What *should* I know about this subject?

Second, write down your questions.
- You may be tempted to skip this step, but don't. It's too easy to forget your questions or to neglect them once you've started reading if you don't write them down.

> Third, seek the answers to your questions as you read.
>
> - So this step *technically* happens *during reading,* but that's okay. While you read, be sure to seek the answers to your questions and to write those down as well.

Actions speak louder than words:

Just Do It:
What do readers look like while Questioning?

Now you can finally put pen to paper. Readers who are questioning will probably spend a bit of time scratching their heads and furrowing their brows, but *then* you will see them writing their questions in the margins of the text, in their notebooks, or on sticky notes.

Later, when they begin reading, you'll see them flip back and forth between their questions and the reading so they can actually take notes on the answers to their questions.

Next Steps

Need I even remind you what the next steps are now? Okay, just for old time's sake:

First, make sure you are asking questions, and then *following through* by seeking the answers to your questions while reading. Over time you should see that this helps improve your comprehension and recall, but if not, then perhaps you are asking the wrong questions. If you're reading for class, pay attention to the sort of questions your instructor asks in class and on tests and quizzes, and try to ask similar questions before you read.

Second, make note of when this skill become automatic. This ongoing self-reflection is an important tool for any reader, because it helps you recognize your strengths and weaknesses so you can continue to improve.

Before Reading:
REVIEW

CONGRATULATIONS! You have now finished learning about the most important ways expert readers approach a text *before* they read. Before we move on, here's some additional information and a review so you can be certain that you have the basics down.

Additional Information: All of the work you do before reading is what we call *frontloading* in the reading world. Want to know something interesting about frontloading? Frontloading is *the most important* thinking you do as a reader because it has the greatest impact on how well you comprehend what you read and how well you recall the information later on. In other words, the things you do before you read are more important than what you do during and after reading, so these skills you just learned (the before reading skills) are going to have the greatest effect on your reading ability.

The during and after reading skills are important as well, of course, and you may find that some of them are more helpful to you than the before reading skills. But in general, the thinking you do before you read sets the tone for how well you are going to read, and sometimes that makes all the difference. Think of your before reading work as your compass; it helps you get your bearings so you know where you are and where you are going before you begin reading.

The good news is that these before reading skills are pretty simple, aren't they? *Anyone* can master these skills. You just have to be willing to put in the time into practicing them until they become habitual ways of thinking about text for you.

Now, a review. Let's see how well you understand and recall what you've read so far:

- Can you name and describe all six before reading skills?
- Which of these before reading skills do you believe you have already mastered?
- Which of these before reading skills do you think you will need to work on most?
- What are the four things you should know about reading, as discussed in the introduction to this book?
- What do I mean when I say the skills are really about developing *ways of thinking?*

Perhaps you should flip back through what you've read so far to make sure that your responses to these questions are accurate. Once you've reviewed, you're ready to move on to the *during reading skills.*

Remember: Now that you know how you should be thinking before you read, you MUST start doing it! It's not enough to know the skills, you have to apply them.

Timeout for Self-Assessment and Reflection

Now that you've been developing new ways of thinking before you read, *(you are using the before reading skills, right? If not, I implore you to stop reading this page and go back right now. This stuff is important!)* it's time to take a step back and assess your current habits and reading ability so you can compare them to where you were when you started reading this book.

Take some time to write down the following information *before* you go back and look at what you wrote during the last Timeout for Self-Assessment. Like last time, keep this information somewhere where you'll be able to find it later so you can marvel at your progress later on.

- The next three or four things you read, note how long it takes you to read them. Then, record the # of pages and your reading time.
- How often do you read something and realize that you don't remember what you just read when you get to the end? Does this happen more often with certain types of readings?
- What do you do when you find an unfamiliar word in the reading? Do you skip it? Look up the definition? Highlight it? Try to figure out its meaning on your own?
- Do you read *every word* in a text, or do you skip words, sentences, or paragraphs?
- If you are reading something that contains charts, pictures, or other special features, do you read them or skip over them?
- What comes to mind when you hear the word *reading?* Be honest!

- In what environment do you read? Is there noise in the background, such as music, television, or other people? Do you have your phone or a computer nearby while you read? Where are you sitting when you read? How is the light?
- How often do you find yourself distracted from a reading? Do you check text messages or Facebook while reading? Do you stop to grab a snack? Do you divide your time between the reading and any other things?
- If you are a student, how well do you do on assignments or tests based on readings that you have read? Do you do poorly even though you read the assigned readings?
- If you are a student, when do you do your assigned readings for class? Do you rush to read them at the last minute, or do you start them early enough so you won't have to rush?

Now, go back and read what you wrote the last time I asked you to do some self-reflecting. Do you see any improvements from last time? Are some things exactly the same? Consider how far you've come and where you'd like to go moving forward, and write down one more piece of information:

- Which specific skills are working for you? Do you want to start using any of the skills even more? Do you have any other thoughts about your reading progress you'd like to note?

Okay, that was more than one piece of information. Please say you'll forgive me.

During Reading:
DEVELOP METACOGNITION

Excuse me? Develop WHAT?

Metacognition is thinking *about* your thinking. In other words, it is the ability to examine your own thinking process in order to make the adjustments necessary to help you better comprehend, retain, and apply the information you're reading.

In addition, developing metacognition:
- Helps you develop a plan before reading
- Helps you monitor your understanding during reading
- Helps you evaluate your thinking after reading and make necessary changes the next time you read

The truth is that you have already been developing your metacognition by working through the *before reading skills* in this book. When I ask you to monitor whether you are applying a skill before reading, what I'm really asking you to do is to think about your thinking. Metacognition during reading shifts your focus to monitoring your thinking while you read.

This is all nice to know, but let's get down to brass tacks:

How do readers develop metacognition during reading?

First, practice your before reading skills.

- When you activate your prior knowledge, preview, predict, question, and set a purpose, you are already developing your metacognition. Great job!

Second, start listening to the voice in your head while reading.

- The voice in your head is there whether or not you've ever noticed it. I call it a "voice" because when I think or read to myself that is what I hear, a voice. However, over the years I've learned from students that not everyone hears a voice—some people see images, some see words, and one student said that when she read to herself she saw an actual movie playing in her mind. Whatever it is that you see or hear while you read, I'm going to call it the voice in your head.
- Pay attention to the voice in your head and start *listening* to it while you read. This may seem distracting at first, and it might be, but trust me on this one. With time, paying attention to the voice in your head will become as automatic as any other skill you've mastered.
- Use the steps on the next page to start monitoring your thinking, which is another way of saying *developing metacognition.*

Develop Metacognition
by Listening to the Voice in Your Head*

1. Read a short article or story and record ***every single thing*** the voice in your head says as you read. I find it easiest to write these thoughts out in the margins of the text itself. If you don't want to write in the actual text, use sticky notes and place them as close to the text as you can.

2. **When you finish reading the piece, go back and label each thought you had while reading as either a USEFUL THOUGHT or a DISTRACTING THOUGHT.** The voice in your head shares two types of thoughts:

   a. **USEFUL THOUGHTS.** These thoughts help you focus on the reading. Examples:
      i. Connect to the text by saying things such as, "Oh, my Aunt Ida used to talk about this!"
      ii. Ask questions about the text by saying things such as, "I wonder why this happens?"
      iii. Give opinions about the text, such as, "This passage seems out of place with the rest of the chapter."
      iv. Talk back to the text by saying things such as, "That is ridiculous! This character would *never* betray his best friend like that."
      v. Remember what is read by saying things such as, "Oh, this concept was also included in Chapter 4, so it must be important."

   b. **DISTRACTING THOUGHTS.** These thoughts cause readers to lose focus. Examples:
      i. Loses track of what is being read by saying things

such as, "I wonder whether Sam will like the shirt I'm wearing today."

ii Strays from the text by saying things such as, "This chapter on precipitation reminds me of that time I went snowboarding and couldn't stand up. Hey, I wonder if Jeremy still snowboards. Maybe I should look him up on Facebook and see. He used to be sponsored, how cool is that? . . . "

iii. Forgets what is read by saying things such as, "Ooh, the cheese fries smell so good today. I wonder if I have enough money to buy some. If not, I'll just borrow from Tanner, he's always generous. Do I still owe him money from last week? . . . "

iv. Doesn't care about the reading. This Inner Voice says things that have nothing at all to do with the reading.

3. If the voice in your head was distracting, redirect your purpose for reading to eliminate the distractions.

a. First: Identify the Distraction

i. If the voice in your head is saying, "That kid sitting behind me is making the most annoying clicking noises with his pen"? Distraction = Annoying kid behind you

ii. Is the voice in your head is saying, "Cheese fries! Cheese fries!"? Distraction = Hunger

iii. If the voice in your head is saying, "I have no idea what this is about" ? Distraction = Lack of comprehension

b. Second: Ignore the Distraction or Eliminate It

   i. Is the distraction out of your control? Do your best to ignore it. (e.g. You can't switch seats in a crowded lecture even though Annoying Guy is still clicking his pen behind you after you asked him to stop.)
   ii. Is the distraction within your control? Eliminate it. (e.g. If the voice in your head won't stop saying "Cheese fries! Cheese fries!" then you're probably just really hungry. Go eat something, *then* come back to your reading.)
   iii. Is the distraction directly related to your comprehension? (e.g. If the voice in your head is saying "I have no idea what this is about" then you just need to take a step back and apply your before reading skills again. See next bullet point . . .)

c. Third: Reset Your Purpose for Reading
   i. Reset your purpose for reading. Remember:
      1. Set clear and measurable goals:
         a. How many annotations (and of what kind) do you plan to make?
         b. How much do you plan to read ~or~ for how long do you plan to read?

d. Fourth and Finally: Regroup and Reread

   i. Regroup: Go back to the reading when you're ready, and start all over again!

I adapted the Voice In Your Head approach from information shared by reading specialist Cris Tovani at a presentation in Lake County, Illinois in 2008, where she discussed her Inner Voice approach to helping students "hold their thinking." Great way to think of it, isn't it? Writing down your thoughts as holding your thinking. *Superb.*

Actions speak louder than words:

Just Do It: What do readers look like while Developing Metacognition?

Metacognitive readers are very active while reading. They take notes, they pause their reading to become aware of their thought process, and then they take more notes as they re-group and continue reading. If they realize that something is distracting them, they eliminate or ignore the distraction and then reset their purpose. You can spot a metacognitive reader by her movement, and by all the notes you'll see scribbled in the margins of her text.

Next Steps

You should know what's coming now:

First, apply this skill. Develop your metacognition every time you read, and celebrate when this skill starts to become easier and more automatic for you.

Second, pay attention to which of the before reading skills you rely on most. Every reader will favor different skills. You may find that activating your prior knowledge and setting a purpose are the most useful skills for you. Pay attention to which skills you use and which you don't use. Make note of this somewhere, so if you one day find yourself struggling while reading something, you will know which skills to try out once more.

For example, predicting may not be very helpful to you in any of your current classes, but you may find that it becomes a very useful tool in a class you take next semester.

During Reading:
IDENTIFY TOPIC AND MAIN IDEA

The **topic** is the common theme or message of a reading. This is the general thing that all of the paragraphs in a piece of reading discuss.

The **main idea** is the key concept that is explored in a text.

Why is it so important to identify the topic and main idea?

The ability to identify the topic and main idea of a piece of writing is a key skill for any reader. Identifying the topic and main idea will allow you to evaluate the reading on a critical level, which is something that you must do as a reader if you plan to apply the knowledge you acquire from reading.

In addition, identifying the topic and main idea:
- Encourages you to read *actively*
- Helps you *self-assess* whether you are comprehending the reading
- Helps guide your reading as you continue through the text by setting expectations for what is to come

The ability to identify the topic and main idea in a piece of reading is really more a *result* of applying reading skills than a reading skill, itself. If you are using the skills we've already discussed, you should be able to identify the topic and main idea of whatever you're reading.

The steps I outline below will be helpful if you find that you are not quite certain that you understand a piece of reading. Additionally, writing the topic and main idea in the margins of everything you read is an excellent study tool—when it comes time to go back and study things you have already read, notes about the topic and main idea of different sections of text will become an excellent study guide.

Additionally, if you are in a class that includes a discussion or lecture about a reading, you will be able to monitor whether you understand the reading based on what you identify as the topic and main idea. If, during a discussion, you find that your understanding of the topic and main idea of a reading has nothing to do with the discussion (or lecture) then it's time to go back and reread.

This is all nice to know, but let's get down to brass tacks:

How do readers identify the topic and main idea during reading?

First, consider what you discovered when you applied your before reading skills.
1. What did you predict about the piece? Were your predictions correct?
2. What did you learn from previewing the piece?
3. What is the larger context in which you're reading this piece—for which class are you reading? Consider how this piece fits into the topic of your class.

Second, identify the topic of the reading.
1. Ask yourself: What is this reading about? The answer is likely the topic of the piece.

> 2. If you're stumped, look to:
>   c. The title
>   d. Any repeated words or ideas
>   e. The common theme or focus that all of the paragraphs or sections have in common
>
> Third, identify the main idea in each paragraph.
> 1. Ask yourself: What is this paragraph about? The answer is likely the main idea of the paragraph.
>   b. If you're stumped, identify:
>   iii. The topic sentence
>   iv. Repeated words or ideas
>   v. How the paragraph supports the topic of the piece

Actions speak louder than words:

Just Do It: What do readers look like while Identifying Topic & Main Idea?

Readers who identify the topic and main idea will likely write in their text itself. They'll put a big box around the main topic of the text or draw big arrows pointing to it. They'll underline supporting details and sentences that state the main idea. They'll scribble their own ideas in the margins. They'll be working hard, that's for sure.

Next Steps

I think we're ready to summarize the Next Steps in three words:
Apply and reflect.
Apply this skill, and reflect on whether it is helpful.

During Reading:
IDENTIFY TEXT STRUCTURES

Text structures refer to the way the writing is organized in a particular piece of reading. There are many ways to organize text, but the most common are:

- Order
- Definition
- Classification
- Compare/contrast
- Cause & effect
- Simple listing

Why is identifying text structures so important (and powerful) for readers?

The ability to identify text structures:

Helps you comprehend and remember the information you're reading

Helps you locate and identify the key concepts in the text, AKA: What kind of notes should I take? What should I be learning?

In other words, identifying the structure of a text will help you understand why the writer shares the information in the reading and why it is important.

Identifying text structures is something that expert readers do without even recognizing it. In other words, I never think to myself, "Oh gee, this text is a classification piece. How wonderful!" In fact, I didn't even recognize the names for the different types of texts until I started teaching students how to recognize text structures. The only time I recommend taking the time to recognize a text structure is when you find yourself reading something that is very difficult for you to comprehend despite using all of the skills I have already discussed in this book.

Identifying a text structure is like using a road map in an unfamiliar place. You only bother to pull out a map if you are having trouble getting around, and you will only need to bother identifying a text's structure if you are having difficulty comprehending the text.

That being said, this is a wonderful tool for navigating difficult texts because it makes the information much more accessible. Once you understand *why* a writer presents information in a certain way, it is easier to understand the information, itself.

This is all nice to know, but let's get down to brass tacks:

How do readers identify text structures during reading?

Order
AKA Chronological order, process, or sequence writing
- Ideas are presented in the order in which they occur (either in time, experience, or another applicable order.)
- Look for transitional words that indicate order, such as *first, second, next, then, meanwhile, last, until,* etc.
- Directions, instructions, and news reports are often written in an order pattern

Definition
- A concept is introduced, defined, then explained using details and examples.
- Look for phrases that indicate definition, such as *is defined as, means, indicates, refers to, is called, etc.*
- Textbooks and instruction manuals often use definition writing.

Classification
- Identifies the major categories within a broad topic
- Look for phrases and words that indicate classification, such as *type, class, group, kinds, divisions, categories,* etc.

- Textbooks often use classification writing to discuss large areas within academic disciplines.

Compare/Contrast
- Ideas are discussed based on their similarities (comparisons) or differences (contrasts)
- Look for phrases and words that indicate compare/contrast, such as *similar, different, however, but, on the other hand, parallels,* etc.

Cause & Effect
- Discusses something that has occurred (event) because of some situation or circumstance (cause)
- Look for phrases that indicate cause & effect, such as *consequently, because, for this reason, therefore, leads to, as a result, due to, thus,* etc.

Simple Listing
- Ideas are presented in a series with supporting details; the order of their presentation is seemingly random
- Look for phrases and words that indicate listing, such as *in addition, another, first, second, next, another, also, too, finally, for example,* etc.

Actions speak louder than words:

Just Do It: What do readers look like while Identifying Text Structures?

While identifying text structures, readers will probably be flipping through their text to compare what and how the piece is written. They'll look for patterns and mark them with a highlighter or their pen, and they'll take notes about what they find while they're doing it.

Next Steps

Apply and reflect. Apply and reflect, my friend.

During Reading:
IDENTIFY TEXT FEATURES and
PAY ATTENTION TO THEM!

Text features are the unique items in a text, the things that are more than plainly written words and sentences on the page.

Examples of text features:
- Book description (usually on front or back cover, or book jacket)
- Table of contents
- Index
- Glossary
- Headings & subheadings
- About the author
- Bold print
- Italic print
- Diagrams/charts/graphs/tables
- Photographs/illustrations
- Captions

Why is it so important for readers to identify text features?

Text features help communicate the information in a text, and oftentimes they share information that is not included in the regular text.

In addition, identifying text features helps you:
- Identify the most important information in a text
- Anticipate what is to come next
- Understand complex ideas
- Find important information

Text features are like accessories; they draw the reader's eye to the most important information in a text, just as when a woman wears earrings and a necklace they draw people's eyes up to her face. When a writer chooses to feature certain text, you can be sure that means she believes it is important, and therefore it's worth noting.

This is all nice to know, but let's get down to brass tacks:

How do readers use text features during reading?

First, consider your purpose for reading.
- What kind of information can these features provide that will help you fulfill your purpose?

Second, consider whether you need extra support to comprehend the reading.
- If the voice in your head is saying things such as, "I don't understand this," consider using text features to deepen your understanding of the reading.

Third, seek out information that's presented in your language.
- If you prefer to see information presenting visually, then images such as pictures or graphic representations might help make more sense to you than the words themselves.

Fourth, consider the author's purpose for featuring the text.
- There must be a reason the author decided to highlight certain information. Figure out why the featured text is more important than the plain text.

Actions speak louder than words:

Just Do It: What do readers look like while Identifying Text Features?

Readers who identify text features keep a sharp eye out for special text. Then, they pause at the featured text to consider why it was featured, and what they should learn from it. They'll take notes about it, or even add their own additional features to it to make sure that they can remember what they thought of its importance while reading.

Next Steps

Apply and reflect.

During Reading:
PREDICT OUTCOMES

Why is it so important to predict outcomes while reading?

The act of predicting outcomes while reading is very powerful, as it keeps readers engaged with the text and encourages readers to monitor their own comprehension while reading. Just as we discussed predicting as a before reading skill, expert readers continue to predict during reading.

Review the section on Predicting in the Before Reading skills if you need a refresher.

This is all nice to know, but let's get down to brass tacks:

How do readers predict outcomes during reading?

Your predictions will vary based on the type of writing that you are reading. Here are some examples of predictions you can make during reading:
- Something specific is going to happen to a character
- The text is going to discuss a particular concept in detail
- The text is going to illustrate the connection between two seemingly different ideas
- My before reading predictions are going to be confirmed or
- disproved

- The author is going to reveal bias towards an idea or character
- The author is going to disprove a commonly held belief
- Any prediction that you make during reading is going to help your comprehension, so get out that crystal ball, and get predicting!

Actions speak louder than words:

Just Do It: What do readers look like while Predicting Outcomes?

Readers who predict outcomes will often flip back through their notes when they come across information about something they predicted. You'll see them stop and then flip back furiously to see what they originally thought would happen. If their prediction was correct, they'll probably smile and give themselves a pat on the back.

Next Steps

Apply and reflect.
Were you expecting me to say something else?

During Reading:
ANNOTATE *AKA* WRITE IN YOUR BOOKS!

When you **annotate,** you make marks in the reading that help you understand, identify important information, remember what you were thinking while reading, and stay engaged with the reading. Recording the voice in your head (from Developing Metacognition) is a form of annotating, as is highlighting, underlining, writing in the margins (AKA writing marginalia), and making any other marks while you read.

Why is it so important to Annotate while reading?

I like to think of annotating as *evidence of thinking*. Your annotations are proof that you are thinking while reading. If you aren't thinking while reading, you won't have anything to write, right? More importantly . . .

Annotating:

- Helps you self-monitor comprehension, which you already know is very important
- Makes a record of your thoughts while reading, which helps you identify areas of confusion, questions, or original ideas
- Keeps you engaged while reading, so it really helps keep distracting thoughts at bay
- Helps you organize the material in a way that makes sense to you

Annotations can also serve as a road map for a reader. That last bullet point says that annotations can help you organize the material in a way that makes sense to you, and this is absolutely true. This is an often overlooked benefit to annotating. If you are reading large blocks of plain text, try marking it up with annotations to help yourself find the important information next time you refer back to it.

How do readers annotate during reading?

During Reading:
Every reader has her own method for annotating which develops over time. I'm going to share my annotations with you to give you concrete examples of the types of annotations you can make, but you should develop your own annotations according to what works best for you.

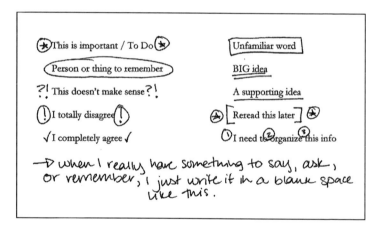

Actions speak louder than words:

Just Do It:
What do readers look like while Annotating?

Annotators are writers. They have a pen in hand, a set of highlighters at their side, and maybe even some colored sticky notes at the ready. You'll know an annotator by the margins of her text; they'll be filled with words and pictures and symbols that only she can decipher.

Annotators never read idly; they are always moving. There is always something to mark, and their pens are always flying.

Next Steps

I bet you thought I was going to say *Apply and Reflect*, didn't you?

Well, I am going to say that, but first . . .

Get yourself some tools for annotating. A simple pen can be enough, but if you have some extra cash to burn and you really like accessories, go nuts! One of my peers from grad school at Appalachian State (GO APPS!) had a veritable buffet of annotation tools—art markers in beautiful colors; every size, color, and shape of sticky note you could imagine; highlighters; *and* colored paperclips in different shapes. She had an elaborate (and bewildering) annotating system that turned all of her notes and textbooks into beautiful, multi-colored little works of art. Even the color and shape of the paperclips that kept notes on certain pages held secret meaning for her.

Once you've set yourself up with annotation tools . . .
Apply and reflect.

During Reading:
REVIEW

CONGRATULATIONS! You have now finished learning about the most important ways of thinking before and during reading. Before we move on, here's some additional information and a review so you can be certain that you have the basics down.

Additional Information: I want to remind you that while these skills require repeated practice in order to become ways of thinking, they *shouldn't* be adding too much time to your reading process. Focus on one skill at a time, and when that skills starts to feel automatic, or at least a bit easier, then it's time to focus on the next skill. Do not attempt to practice every single skill every single time you read.

Now, a review. Let's see how well you understand and recall what you've read so far:

- Can you name and describe all six during reading skills?
- Which of these during reading skills do you believe you have already mastered?
- Which of these during reading skills do you think you will need to work on most?
- Can you name and describe all six before reading skills? Have you already incorporated most of them into your new ways of thinking as a reader?

Perhaps you should flip back through what you've read so far to make sure that your responses to these questions are accurate. Once you've reviewed, you're ready to move on to the *during and after reading skills.*

Remember: Now that you know how you should be thinking before and during reading, you MUST start doing it! It's not enough to know the skills; you have to apply them.

Timeout for Self-Assessment and Reflection

Now you are heading into the most rewarding aspect of reading: reading critically. You have at least a foundational knowledge about all of the most important *before* and *during* reading skills, and now you're ready to not only understand what you read, but to critique it as well. Have I told you that reading just gets better and better?

Now, before we move on to the next set of skills, take some time to write down the following information. Like last time, keep this information somewhere where you'll be able to find it later so you can marvel at your progress later on.

- The next three or four things you read, note how long it takes you to read them. Then, record the # of pages and your reading time.
- How often do you read something and realize that you don't remember what you just read when you get to the end? Does this happen more often with certain types of readings?
- What do you do when you find an unfamiliar word in the reading? Do you skip it? Look up the definition? Highlight it? Try to figure it out on your own?
- Do you read *every word* in a text, or do you skip words, sentences, or paragraphs?
- If you are reading something that contains charts, pictures, or other special features, do you read them or skip over them?
- What comes to mind when you hear the word *reading?* Be honest!
- In what environment do you read? Is there noise in the

background, such as music, television, or other people? Do you have your phone or a computer nearby while you read? Where are you sitting when you read? How is the light?

- How often do you find yourself distracted from a reading? Do you check text messages or Facebook while reading? Do you stop to grab a snack? Do you divide your time between the reading and any other things?
- If you are a student, how well do you do on assignments or tests based on readings that you have read? Do you do poorly even though you read the assigned readings?
- If you are a student, when do you do your assigned readings for class? Do you rush to read them at the last minute, or do you start them early enough so you won't have to rush?

Now, go back and read what you wrote the last time I asked you to do some self-reflecting. Do you see any improvements from last time? Are some things exactly the same? Consider how far you've come and where you'd like to go moving forward, and write down the following:

- Which specific skills are working for you? Do you want to start using any of the skills even more? Do you have any other thoughts about your reading progress you'd like to note?

You should be seeing some significant improvement in your reading skills by now. If not, it's time to figure out *why.* My best guess is that you aren't truly putting these skills to work for yourself. If this is the case, do some reviewing before you move on.

During & After Reading:
CRITICAL READING: AN INTRODUCTION

Critical readers go beyond mere comprehension to *analyze, judge,* and *interpret* texts. To do this, critical readers examine not only *what* is written but *how* and *why* it is written. This means that critical readers do more than simply *understand* what they read; they *engage* with the text in order to discover new levels of meaning and new ways to apply the text to issues and ideas beyond the page.

It is vital that you understand a text's basic meaning, but in order to get the most out of your reading, you must become a critical reader. Critical readers access a text's true meaning and value, and they get far more out of their reading than those who only read for base-level comprehension.

Here's a little secret: I strongly believe that many people who say they hate reading only feel that way because they've never developed critical reading skills, so an entire world of meaning is inaccessible to them. Of course they hate reading! They aren't really getting much out of reading. If you sat through a two-hour play that was performed in a language you don't speak, you probably wouldn't enjoy the experience. This is exactly what happens to basic readers, so it's no surprise to me at all when they say they don't like reading. I imagine I wouldn't like it either if I didn't get much out of it.

Critical Reading vs. Close Reading

When I discuss critical reading I'm referring to close examination of nonfiction texts. I would use the term *close reading* when referring to close examination of literary texts. Close reading is reading a piece of literature to analyze the meaning and significance of the details chosen for use in the text.

We won't spend much time discussing close reading in this book, as it is outside of our purpose. You will learn to do close reading should you choose to take literature courses in college (Which I highly recommend you do, by the way). *However,* most of the skills we discuss in this book can and will help you read fiction, as well.

During & After Reading: DISTINGUISH BETWEEN FACT AND OPINION

A **fact** is a statement of actuality based on evidence, experience, or observation

An **opinion** is a statement of belief, judgment, or feeling. Opinions are an individual's views on a subject.

Why is it so important to distinguish between fact and opinion when reading?

You must be able to distinguish between fact and opinion when reading because this determination will help you figure out if you accept the author's assertions about the subject. In addition, when it comes time for you to evaluate a piece of reading, you need a clear understanding of whether the author is dealing in facts or opinions before you can draw your own conclusions about the piece.

This is all nice to know, but let's get down to brass tacks:

How do readers distinguish between fact and opinion during reading?

First, think back to what kind of piece you're reading and the author's purpose:
This should give you a big clue as to whether the information *should be* fact or opinion. A chapter from your biology textbook is likely to be filled with facts, while an editorial about a politician currently running for office is likely to be filled with opinions.

Second, look for clues in the author's word choice:
- Words that interpret, label, or express emotion indicate that you are probably reading an opinion: *pretty, dangerous, evil, good, vehemently, etc.*
- Words and phrases that indicate statements of opinion: *probably, perhaps, I believe,*
I think, I feel, I suggest, etc.
- Words that indicate the use of evidence as support indicate that you might be reading factual information: *according to, the evidence supports, as stated by, the research proves, etc.*

Third, determine the author's authority:
- Is the author an expert on the subject? Not sure? Consult the Internet to see if you can find anything about her background or other published works.
- Does the author have the skill or experience to support her claims?

- Does the author cite authorities to support his claims? Are they *really* authorities? Time to get back on Google if you're not sure.

Finally, examine the major assertions the author makes:
- Do they make sense?
- Are they presented in an objective manner?
- Do they actually support the author's view?
- Do they *prove* the point, or simply support that it could *reasonably* be true?

Actions speak louder than words:

Just Do It:
What do readers look like while distinguishing between fact and opinion?

When trying to distinguish between fact and opinion, readers are probably annotating the author's assertions and then doing some Googling or research at the local library to figure out whether they're based on fact or opinion. Sometimes, it won't take more than a few seconds to figure this out, but sometimes it may take considerably more time. The more background information you have about the writer and the piece, the easier this step will be. (In other words: Those before reading skills are really going to help you out here.)

Next Steps

Begin getting into the habit of making an annotation whenever you see words or phrases that indicate fact or opinion. You can create your own special symbol for facty phrases (maybe F! in a box next to the phrase) and opiniony (OP!)

phrases. Have fun with it; your annotations are just for you. Then, of course, reflect on how well you're applying this skill as you go on. If you realize that you mistook something for fact when it was opinion, make note of that and go back to the text to see which clues you missed, then use that experience to help you do better next time.

During & After Reading:
READ CRITICALLY:
IDENTIFY AUTHOR'S PURPOSE

Have you noticed that we've discussed *purpose* a couple times now? Let's dig a bit deeper into purpose:

There are *basically* six main purposes for writing:
- Writing for personal expression (journals, diaries, poetry)
- Writing to express a message (poetry, the spoken word)
- Writing to affect the reader (advertisements, personal statements, editorials)
- Writing to inform (movie reviews, how-to pieces, text-books)
- Writing to Connect, AKA Social writing (letters, notes, text messages, emails)
- Writing to comment on other writing (preface to a book, reviews, feedback on essays)

A writer can have multiple purposes for writing, as well. Not everything has to fall under just one of these categories.

Why is it so important to identify the author's purpose?

In order to truly understand a piece of writing, readers must understand the why the author bothered to write in the first place. Once you understand the author's purpose for writing, her message will be *much* easier to identify, which will make it easier for you to respond to what you read.

This is all nice to know, but let's get down to brass tacks:

How do readers identify the author's purpose?

First, consider which of the six types of writing you are reading (see above).
Consider:
- *Why are you reading this, anyway?* If it's for a class, then the context in which the reading was assigned should give you a good idea of its purpose. Is it a textbook chapter? Then the purpose is probably to inform. Is it a political speech made by a candidate right before election time? Then the purpose is probably to persuade listeners to vote a certain way, AKA to affect the reader.
- Where was this piece originally published? Different publications have different purposes, and they aren't that difficult to ascertain if you spend a couple minutes checking out the source.
- Who is the intended audience?
- Who is the author? Do you know anything about her that might give you clues as to why she wrote this piece?

Second, identify the main idea (which you've already done, I'm sure):
- The main idea should give you some insight into the author's purpose. Is it:
- An argument?
- An observation?
- A message?

- An emotional plea?
- A judgment call?

Once you've identified the author's purpose, determine whether the author succeeded in meeting her purpose and ultimately, whether you agree with her:
- Are you satisfied with the information provided?
- Do you agree or disagree with this piece?
- If you disagree, what is missing?
- If you agree, why?

Your growing critical reading skills will help you with this last step.

Just Do It:
What do readers look like while identifying the author's purpose?

This is the point in the reading process where it gets even more difficult to isolate one skill from another. You just learned about *distinguishing between fact and opinion*, and in many ways *identifying the author's purpose* could be considered another way to do just that. What you're doing here is reading critically, and it usually looks like plain old reading, perhaps with a furrowed brow or a hand poised thoughtfully at your chin. And keep talking to other people who are reading the same text as you. If you're a student, call, text, or email someone from class and compare thoughts on the reading.

Next Steps

Now that you've been introduced to this skill, you should *always* try to identify the author's purpose for writing. You know that old cliché where a husband brings home flowers and his wife is immediately suspicious that he's done something wrong? That's a perfect illustration of someone digging beyond the surface to figure out the purpose behind the gesture. I guess my point is: Be the suspicious wife whenever you're reading something important.

During & After Reading:
READ CRITICALLY:
IDENTIFY GENERALIZATIONS

A **generalization** is a conclusion that is drawn and applied to a large group.

Why is it so important to identify generalizations?

The ability to identify generalizations in reading helps readers evaluate the text for underlying assumptions and draw their own conclusions and opinions about the subject.

People often generalize, and my guess is that you've probably heard some about yourself over the years. Humor me for a minute and be honest about what pops into your head when you read the following descriptions:

- She loves to read
- He attends community college
- She loves cheese fries and wishes she could eat them every day.

If you think people who love to read are nerdy and smart, those are generalizations that you're applying to an entire group: readers. If you think people who attend community college are bad students, that is a generalization you're applying to an entire group: community college students. If you think people who love cheese fries must be overweight, there's another generalization.

These things may be true of readers, community college students, and people who love cheese fries. But then again, they may not be true at all. The reason you need to identify generalizations when you read is so you can remind yourself to be open to the possibility that the generalization a writer has made *may not be accurate.*

This is all nice to know, but let's get down to brass tacks:

How do readers identify generalizations during reading?

First, take another look at the main idea of the piece.

- What is the purpose of the reading? Would generalizations about a particular group help support the author's purpose?
- Is the author trying to persuade or argue a point? If so, keep an eye out for generalizations in the writing.

Second, examine the language.

- Examples of words and phrases that often indicate generalizations are:
  - All, always, most, everyone, sometimes, never, seldom, few, in general, generally, overall.

Third, identify the generalizations, and their validity.

- What is the author generalizing?
  - Consider how this generalization might serve the author's purpose.
  - Does this generalization seem valid based on everything else you know about this group?
    - Look at the examples provided to support the generalization, and remain open to the possibility that the author might be incorrect.

Actions speak louder than words:

Just Do It:
What do readers look like while identifying generalizations?

This is where you continue that brow furrowing and chin holding I described last time. If you have a mustache you might find yourself twirling the ends of it in between your fingers at this point.

Next Steps

Whenever you find yourself questioning whether an author's assertions are valid or true, that's a good time to check for generalizations. This isn't something you will have to do *every time* you read; rather, you'll identify generalizations when you find yourself reading something that warrants a more critical eye.

During & After Reading:
READ CRITICALLY: IDENTIFY BIAS

Bias is a judgment based on personal opinion, beliefs, or experiences. When an author writes with bias, her opinion on the issue is so strong that she only fairly represents one side of the issue.

Identifying bias serves a similar purpose as *identifying generalizations:* You, the reader, are digging deeper to make sure that the author isn't misrepresenting or, at the very least, underrepresenting certain information or ideas because of personal beliefs or experiences.

Remember way back when you started reading this book and we discussed *prior knowledge?* Well, authors have their own set of prior knowledge, and sometimes (some might argue *always*) that prior knowledge affects the way they present information in their writing. Critical readers are not only aware of the way their own experiences, beliefs, and feelings affect their reading; they keep a sharp eye out for the author's, as well.

Why is it so important to identify bias?

The ability to identify bias in reading is essential so readers can draw fair and objective conclusions. It's important to note that bias does not always lead to incorrect information in text. However, readers can only draw accurate conclusions after identifying bias and *then* evaluating whether the bias skews the information presented to the point of inaccuracy.

As a reader, you bring your own biases to any reading you do. In addition to identifying an author's bias, it's important that you identify your own, as well. If you find you have preconceived notions about a text before you even read it, then it's likely that you are bringing bias to the reading. Don't fall into the trap of dismissing a piece of text without first evaluating it.

This is all nice to know, but let's get down to brass tacks:

How do readers identify bias during reading?

First, identify the main idea of the piece.
- Is it a statement of opinion or fact? (You already know how to distinguish between the two!)
- If it is a statement of opinion, consider:
  - Does the author represent both sides of the issue objectively and fairly?
    - If yes, then the writing is likely more or less free from bias.
    - If no, then the writing is likely biased. THEN, carefully evaluate the evidence presented for accuracy.

Actions speak louder than words:

Just Do It:
What do readers look like while identifying bias?

Those *deep thoughts* poses that I described in the last few skills still pretty much apply here, wouldn't you say? You're bending in, reading the pages closely, and probably squinting, deep in thought.

Next Steps

I'm going to lay it all out there and share something with you: This is usually the point in the book when some students in my reading classes, who were otherwise doing very well, start to bail on me. After some time I learned that it isn't because they are just plain *tired* of talking about reading, even though some are. And that's okay.

The reason this is where I start to lose some students is because the *critical reading* section is where the skills start to get messy. *Prior knowledge, connections, purpose*—these things are all pretty straightforward and relatively easy to do. Furthermore, you could practice all of the before reading skills without even cracking open a book, and the during reading skills focused on identifying things that were right there on the page once you *did* open the book.

But now we are several skills into *critical reading* and you might be thinking *this is hard!* You might even find yourself reading and rereading things without being able to understand them as well as you'd like. Trust me when I tell you that *this is normal, and it is going to be okay.*

How do I know it's normal? I've been working with students

in reading classes for a decade, and I've seen it happen over and over again.

How do I know it's going to be okay? I know it's going to be okay because, as I shared at the beginning of this book, *reading is a process, and all it takes to become a better reader.* As long as you are still willing to put in the time, then you are going to get there. So stick with me. Don't bail on me now.

Keep on practicing your skills, and keep on reflecting.

And when you're ready, continue reading this book.

During & After Reading:
READ CRITICALLY: IDENTIFY TONE

Tone refers the mood of a piece of writing, or the emotion that it conveys. An easy way to think about tone is to think about *tone of voice*, which can be angry, sad, happy, sarcastic, etc.

Why is it so important to identify tone?

Recognizing the tone of a text is an important skill for critical readers because it requires the reader to interpret the text and to make inferences about its meaning based on the author's word choices. Once a reader recognizes the tone of a piece, its meaning can become very clear. In other words, like bias and generalizations and purpose, *tone* is just another piece of the puzzle.

It can be very difficult to identify the tone of a piece if you don't have enough background information about tone. To help you flesh out this idea of tone, here's a comparison of things we use to identify tone in person vs. in text:

In Person:
- Facial expressions
- Voice—volume, pitch, etc.
- Body language—posture, etc.

In Text:
- Words
- Punctuation
- Text features

This is all nice to know, but let's get down to brass tacks:

How do readers identify tone during reading?

First, identify *loaded words:* words or phrases in the writing that are intense or emotionally charged.

- Most writers choose their words very carefully. Words and phrases can have **positive, negative,** or **neutral** connotation (connotation refers to a word's emotional impact).

Second, identify whether the words typically have a positive or negative connotation.

- Examples of words with a generally positive connotation: *flower, loving, home*
- Examples of words with a generally negative connotation: *livid, fired, irritating*

Third, identify the author's purpose and use it to identify the tone of the piece.

- The tone of a piece of writing can be described using many words. Here are a few:
  - Respectful, Indignant, Amused, Reverent, Formal, Spiteful, Suspicious, Admiring

Now, here's an important note about tone: See above where I list *home* as an example of a word with positive connotation? Well, here's the thing about words, they mean different things to different people. Someone who lived in an abusive home throughout her childhood may not regard *home* as a word with positive connotation. Similarly, someone who hates her job may think the word *fired* is the loveliest in the universe.

Does this mean that you can never identify tone, then? No, of course not. But it does mean that you should be sure to examine your own assumptions about certain words that hold particular emotion for you and to try to recognize when your personal reaction to certain words might differ from the average reaction, or that of the author's.

Actions speak louder than words:

Just Do It:
What do readers look like while identifying tone?

You might have that trusty highlighter out, boxing *loaded words* while you read so you can examine them later.

Next Steps

Identifying the tone of a piece of writing should become something you do without giving much thought to it, but when you find yourself reading a particularly challenging text or if you find yourself scratching your head unable to figure out what it is you're missing about a text, then it's time to work on identifying the tone of the piece.

During & After Reading:
READ CRITICALLY: RECOGNIZE VALIDITY

Validity refers to the strength of the ideas presented in the reading. A piece of writing with strong support for its ideas has strong validity, whereas writing with weak support for its ideas has weak validity.

An easy way to think about validity is to think about a driver's license. (Just run with me here for a second, okay?) What does it mean to have a valid driver's license? It means the driver's license legally belongs to the person in possession of it and that all of the information on that license is correct. In other words, it has solid, accurate support for everything written on it.

Why is it so important to recognize validity?

The ability to recognize the validity of a writer's ideas is vital for readers to read critically. In order to decide how to use the information in a text or how to respond to it, a reader must first determine whether the ideas are valid. This skill is particularly useful for readers who have to find support for research papers or projects.

This is all nice to know, but let's get down to brass tacks:

How do readers recognize validity during reading?

First, identify the major assertions in the writing.
- What are the ideas or arguments that the writer is putting forth in her writing?
  - Look to the purpose and main idea of the piece if you need help identifying this.

Second, identify the supporting details.
- What information does the author use to support her major assertions?
  - Are these supporting details based on fact or opinion?
  - Can you verify that the supporting details are fact?
  - Is the source reliable?

Third, draw conclusions about the validity of the writing.
- Are you satisfied that the writer is herself a valid source or that the sources she cites are valid?
- If not, seek out information to confirm or deny the validity of her ideas.

By now I hope you're starting to get a sense of déjà vu, because all of the bullet points I've just listed rely on skills we've previously discussed.

Actions speak louder than words:

Just Do It:
What do readers look like while identifying tone?

This is more of the same: You are reading closely, you might be flipping around the text or fact-checking on the Internet. Whatever your particular style, you look good doing it. Keep it up.

Next Steps

It will generally be apparent to you whether a text is a reliable source of information, so don't feel like you have to become a bouncer and check every text's ID when you read. The times to be vigilant about recognizing validity are when you find yourself confused by a text because the information in it doesn't seem to line up with other texts that you've read or when you are looking for texts to use to support an argument in something that you, yourself, are writing, such as a research paper or speech for a class.

Timeout for Self-Assessment and Reflection

You have just reached another milestone on your journey toward becoming a skilled reader; congratulations! You are now in the final stretch.

This part should seem old hat by now. Like last time, keep this information somewhere where you'll be able to find it later so you can marvel at your progress later on.

- The next three or four things you read, note how long it takes you to read them. Then, record the # of pages and your reading time.
- How often do you read something and realize that you don't remember what you just read when you get to the end? Does this happen more often with certain types of readings?
- What do you do when you find an unfamiliar word in the reading? Do you skip it? Look up the definition? Highlight it? Try to figure it out on your own?
- Do you read *every word* in a text, or do you skip words, sentences, or paragraphs?
- If you are reading something that contains charts, pictures, or other special features, do you read them or skip over them?
- What comes to mind when you hear the word *reading?* Be honest!
- In what environment do you read? Is there noise in the background, such as music, television, or other people? Do you have your phone or a computer nearby while you read? Where are you sitting when you read? How is the light?

- How often do you find yourself distracted from a reading? Do you check text messages or Facebook while reading? Do you stop to grab a snack? Do you divide your time between the reading and any other things?
- If you are a student, how well do you do on assignments or tests based on readings that you have read? Do you do poorly even though you read the assigned readings?
- If you are a student, when do you do your assigned readings for class? Do you rush to read them at the last minute, or do you start them early enough so you won't have to rush?

Now, go back and read what you wrote the last time I asked you to do some self-reflecting. Do you see any improvements from last time? Are some things exactly the same? Consider how far you've come and where you'd like to go moving forward, and write down the following:

- Which specific skills are working for you? Do you want to start using any of the skills even more? Do you have any other thoughts about your reading progress you'd like to note?

You should be seeing some significant improvement in your reading skills by now. If not, it's time to figure out *why*. My best guess is that you aren't truly putting these skills to work for yourself. If this is the case, do some reviewing before you move on.

You Have Now Reached the After Reading Skills Portion of Our Program

You've come a long way, my friend. By now you have developed habits that expert readers possess, and you should be enjoying the benefits: you no longer have to reread things four times to understand them, you are likely reading much faster with better comprehension, and you might even be *enjoying* reading a little bit. Fine, maybe not, but a girl can dream. But aren't you enjoying it even a little bit?

The after reading skills are just what they sound like—things skilled readers do after reading. In the scheme of things, they are the habits and skills that are going to help you *retain* the information you read and, if necessary, communicate it to others. These abilities will be especially useful for you if you're a student and find yourself taking tests or engaging in class discussions about assigned readings.

At this point, many of the **before** and **during reading skills** should feel like natural ways of thinking about text, things that you do automatically while reading. Take a moment to celebrate how far you've come as a reader, because you've put in a lot of work to get here.

Now, on to the final skills.

After Reading:
RETELL

Why is it so important to retell after reading?

Retelling is a great way to check your own comprehension after reading.

Remember when I introduced the Do I Get It? App and I told you that it was your first step in becoming independent? You have learned many more skills since then, and now here we are discussing retelling, which is pretty much the *best way* for a reader to independently check her own comprehension.

In addition, retelling:
- Helps you commit the information you just read to memory
- Helps you identify possible gaps in your understanding of complex ideas or texts
- Helps you identify the main idea in a passage based on the information that most stands out to you
- Is one of the *best* study strategies I know. When you retell, you are requiring yourself to recall information from the text without looking at it. Unlike using notecards or looking at your notes, retelling is a great way to identify holes in your understanding about a particular concept.

I highly recommend you start using retelling as a regular study method. Use the information you *did not* recall to create your study guide or notecards, because those missing pieces are the things on which you should focus when studying.

This is all nice to know, but let's get down to brass tacks:

How do readers retell after reading?

When you finish reading a particularly challenging or important text, try the following:

- If you're alone or working with your study group, pause and simply explain (out loud) the gist of what you just read.
- If you can't say it aloud, jot down your retelling in the margin notes of your text, in your notebook, or on a spare receipt in your wallet.

Next, check for gaps in your understanding:

- Refer back to the text—did you miss any large pieces of information?
- Did you adequately identify the main idea in your retelling?
- Were you able to define the major concepts in the reading?

Finally, practice retelling in class, if possible:

- Talk to that cute guy or girl who sits in front of you and ask if you can summarize last night's reading. Answer questions about the reading in class, if the opportunity arises. This will help you retain the information, as well.

Actions speak louder than words:

Just Do It:
What do readers look like while retelling?

You will either be speaking or writing. Retelling takes very little time, I'd say a minute tops, but the one thing you really should do is say it aloud or write it down. Don't just sit there and do a retell in your head, because you will be far more likely to identify gaps in your understanding if you can see them on paper or if you can hear them as you speak aloud.

Next Steps

Unlike some previous skills, this is one that I recommend you practice *every single time you read*. Okay, I take that back—no need to do a retelling of what you read on Facebook; once is more than enough. But whenever you're reading for school, for work, or for some other serious purpose, take a minute and retell whenever you pause in your reading.

Retelling is, as I wrote earlier, an excellent study strategy. If you find yourself cramming for exams, retells are your best friend. Don't waste time going over information you know well. Instead, skim through the text that will be covered in the exam, do a retelling of every major section, and then focus only on the parts that you weren't able to remember in your retelling. This strategy is bound to save you huge amounts of time that you might otherwise waste writing up notecards for concepts that you already know well enough.

After Reading:
REREAD

Why is it so important to reread after reading?

Rereading is a great technique if you finish reading and realize that you have an incomplete understanding of the text. Even if you do feel that you have a complete understanding of the text, rereading can be a great study tool for particularly difficult or dense sections of reading.

Consider rereading *if:*
* You find yourself at the end of a passage with little or no idea of what you just read
* The reading was very difficult and it is important that you have a firm understanding of it because you will be required to apply it in class or elsewhere
* You *thought* you understood the reading, but you went to class and had a difficult time keeping up with the lecture/activity/lesson based on the reading.
* The information is very important, and you aren't sure that you understood all of it after reading the first time through.
* Your annotations have more questions marks than comments.

What if rereading does not improve comprehension or retention?
* If this happens to you, then it's time to revisit those before and during reading skills.
  * Pay very close attention to activating prior knowledge, setting a purpose, and developing metacognition. Be sure to do each of these, and apply them to

your rereading. If you are still stumped, perhaps it's time to beef up your prior knowledge of the subject of the reading before you reread it once again.

Actions speak louder than words:

Just Do It:
What do readers look like while rereading?
Do I really have to write it out? You're reading text and doing all of the wonderful things you've worked so hard to turn into habits.

Next Steps

Pay attention to the things you need to reread. If you find yourself in need of rereading text over and over again for a particular class, then perhaps it's time to set up a meeting with your teacher or professor to get some extra insight into the subject matter or advice about other texts that might help you with that particular class.

After Reading:
MAKE JUDGMENTS & DRAW CONCLUSIONS

Why is it so important to make judgments and draw conclusions after reading?

Drawing conclusions and making judgments about what you read is a vital step for any reader who plans to *apply* the information he reads. As discussed earlier, it is not enough to simply *know* information; skilled readers *apply* information. One major step in applying information is drawing conclusions about it so you can determine whether you agree or disagree, whether it is useful, and how you can use it.

It's probably safe to say that most people make judgments and draw conclusions on a daily basis. If you drive, you constantly judge whether it is safe to make your next move—is it safe to accelerate? Can I change lanes now? Is there enough time for me to make this left turn? Once you judge that a move is safe and decide to make that move, there's your conclusion: I'm going to accelerate now, change lanes, make this left turn.

We also judge and draw conclusions about the people we encounter every day. When I say this to my students the response is almost always the same: They say *they* don't judge, but everyone else judges them. I understand that *judging* has a negative connotation for most people (look at me, throwing around words we've recently discussed).

The fact is that not only is it *not* always a negative thing to judge others and draw conclusions about them; it's actually a *necessary* thing to do. Think back to my example about driving your car. If you didn't judge the situation on the road, you probably wouldn't get too far. Now think about this scenario: Your English professor tells you to partner up with a classmate for a large project. You should probably assess your potential partner and make sure that she seems like the type of student who will follow through and complete her part of the work. Or what about walking out to your car at night in a nearly-empty parking lot? If a group of strangers approaches you yelling obscenities, it's probably a good time to make a judgment call: *these people look a bit out of control,* and draw a conclusion: *they might be dangerous, and I need to get out of here, fast.*

This is all nice to know, but let's get down to brass tacks:

How do readers make judgments and draw conclusions after reading?

First, consider what you've already determined about the reading:

- Is the author a valid source?
- Is she biased?
- Did the author fulfill her purpose?
- What is the tone of the piece?

These should be things you have already considered by now.

Next, reflect on this information:

- What do *you* think about the main idea of the writing?
- Do you agree or disagree?
- Is it useful?
- How can you use this information that you just read?

Finally, draw some conclusions:
- Write out your responses to the questions from the last step. Consider them for a bit, and explore your own opinions about the piece.
- Once you've done this, read your own conclusions to check for bias and validity. We *all* have biases, after all .

Actions speak louder than words:

Just Do It:
What do readers look like while making judgments and drawing conclusions?

Working through the steps above will take you a few minutes of thinking and jotting down your notes. Maybe you'll flip through the text a bit, maybe you'll stroke that fabulous mustache. The details are up to you.

Next Steps

The best scenario at this point is to share your thoughts about the reading with someone else who has also read it. If you're a student, this is where your study buddies come in handy. If you don't know anyone who is reading the text, consult the Internet. There are a lot of people out there with opinions, and many of them like to share them. If you're reading a book, you'll find reviews on Amazon.com, Goodreads.com, Shelfari.com, and Librarything.com, to name a few sites. If you're reading an article, many publications have websites with comment sections under their articles, so check those out, too.

After Reading:
INFER

An **inference** is an idea that is implied in the writing. Unlike literal ideas, which are explicitly stated, inferences are suggested by the writer and thus a bit more difficult to identify than literal ideas.

Cartoons or jokes often use inferences to express their meaning—the punch line doesn't explicitly state what is funny; rather, it implies the joke and relies on the reader's ability to infer meaning in order to "get" it.

Why is it so important to make inferences after reading?

Most writing meant for adults relies on the reader's ability to make inferences in order to understand the true meaning of the piece. If readers do not make inferences about the writing, they often fail to grasp the intended *meaning* of a text, as well as the intended *feeling* of a text. Therefore, inferring is an essential skill for readers who want to fully understand what they're reading.

Have you ever found yourself sitting in a classroom with little idea what the teacher or students are talking about *even though* you read the assignment? If so, it's likely that you just missed the implied meaning of the piece. When I taught high school I once asked my students to read some articles from the news publication *The Onion* for homework, but I made the mistake of neglecting to inform them that *The Onion* is satire. The next day I had a classroom full of very confused sophomores. I thought the articles were hilarious, but the joke was completely lost on my students because they had no idea that they were meant to be funny. *(Of course, had they activated their prior knowledge before reading, they probably would have learned that* The Onion *is satire, but I digress.)*

This is all nice to know, but let's get down to brass tacks:

How do readers make inferences after reading?

First, consider what you've already determined about the reading:
- All of the work you have already done to determine the author's purpose, the validity of the writing, the tone, etc. will help you make inferences about the reading.
- Did you already "get" the implied meaning of the text? Do you already believe you understand what the author is really trying to say? If so, great! You can double-check your understanding in the next steps.

Next, consider the language once again:
- In addition to connotative words and phrases, does the writing have any:
  - Euphemisms (polite ways of saying harsh things)
  - Overly correct language
  - Figurative language

Finally, examine the language for meaning:
- Euphemisms and overly correct language are often hiding harsher realities than what initially appears
- Figurative language (metaphors, similes, idioms, etc.) expresses ideas beyond the literal meaning. (We will discuss this soon!)

Actions speak louder than words:

Just Do It:
What do readers look like while making inferences?

By now, you should have your groove down while reading, and since every reader is different, I can no longer claim to know what you look like at this point. You should be doing your thang in your reading zone and moving along at a good pace by now.

Eventually, you will make inferences while reading without even thinking about it. You may be doing this already. However, if you find yourself completely lost after reading *even though* you understand the words on the page, that's a sign that you're missing the implied meaning of the text, so this skill can help you there.

Next Steps

Check in with others reading the text, and see if your inferences are correct. If you're a student, this part is easy. If you're not reading for school, check out what the collective voices on the good old Internet have to say.

After Reading:
IDENTIFY USE OF IMAGERY & FIGURATIVE LANGUAGE

Authors use **imagery** to create impressions of the five senses in their writing. Imagery helps readers identify the sights, sounds, feelings, tastes, and smells of what the writing describes.

Authors use **figurative language** to evoke images and reactions in readers, as well. Figurative language creates new meanings from words by describing things figuratively, or beyond the literal level. Good figurative language conveys an idea better and stronger than literal language.

Why is it so important to identify use of imagery and figurative language after reading?

Similar to the importance of making inferences, identifying imagery and figurative language in writing is essential for readers who want to understand the true meaning and feeling of the piece. In addition, imagery and figurative language help support a reader's understanding because it helps the reader experience the world of the writing.

This is all nice to know, but let's get down to brass tacks:

How do readers identify use of imagery and figurative language after reading?

Imagery

Imagery relies on words that stimulate the reader's

mind to experience the sensory world of the writing. Examples:

- Red cheeks, tapping of the keys, nubby old sweater, sweet licorice, the heavy smell of apple cider hanging in the air

Similes

A type of figurative language, simile makes an indirect comparison between two things. (You may remember learning that similes often use *like* or *as*.) Examples:

- She was as white as sheet of paper; Life is like a box of chocolates.

Metaphors

Another type of figurative language, metaphors make a direct comparison between two things. Examples:

- She is the apple of my eye; All the world's a stage.

Other commonly used figurative language:

- Idioms: Expressions that do not make literal sense but have an accepted figurative meaning. ("It's raining cats and dogs.")
- Hyperbole: Exaggerations or overstatements. ("I'm freezing!")
- Personification: Attributing human characteristics to nonhuman things. ("The ice crept down the sides of the house.")

Actions speak louder than words:

Just Do It:
What do readers look like while identifying
use of imagery and figurative language?

Same as always, readers identifying imagery and figurative language will be in their reading groove, doing whatever it is they do.

Next Steps

If you find yourself lost, scan the text for language that might be figurative rather than literal. Once you identify figurative language, determine what it means by thinking about the author's word choice. If you can't figure it out, do some digging around—ask your friends, consult the all-knowing Google. Then, think about why the author made the choice to use imagery or figurative language in each particular instance and what that choice says about the message she hopes to convey.

After Reading:
RESPOND

A **reading response** is a summary of the reader's response to what she has read.

Why is it so important to respond after reading?

As we've discussed many times before, it is one thing to understand information, but it is an entirely different thing to be able to apply it. A reading response is the first step in applying the information that you've read. When you take the time to respond to a reading, you take the time to organize your thoughts about it and to put them down in writing. This will not only help you understand what you read, but it will also help you identify *how well* you understand the piece, and it will help you *retain* the information you gleaned from it.

This is all nice to know, but let's get down to brass tacks:

How do readers write responses after reading?

First, consider your responses to the reading:
- Look back at your annotations and identify the responses you had to the reading while you were reading it.

Second, consider this: So, what?
- Focus your response on something interesting. In other words: identify an original idea you had in response to the reading and write about *that*.

Third, connect your response to the reading, itself:
- Be sure to connect your response to the text itself. Consider the author's purpose, point of view, main idea, etc. when writing your response.

Finally, write it down!
- The response doesn't truly exist until you put it to paper. Write it down, let it sit for a while, share it with friends, and add or redirect your response as necessary. You know by now that I'm a big proponent of writing down your thoughts, and there's good reason for it: Once you write them down, it's harder for them to just disappear. How many times have you had an important thought and then *poof!* it flies out of your head a minute or an hour later? I thought so. That's why you should write it down.

Actions speak louder than words:

Just Do It: What do readers look like while responding to reading?

Readers writing responses will be flipping through their annotations and notes, maybe talking aloud to themselves or friends, and ultimately, they'll be *writing.*

Next Steps

Keep it simple. Every time you read something that is important (e.g. an assigned class reading) take five minutes when you're finished and jot down a quick response at the end of the piece. If it's a particularly difficult piece of text, maybe you want to stop every five pages or so and jot down a quick response. I'm not suggesting you sit down at a computer and compose a formal, typed reading response, here. What I'm suggesting is you write a quick response for yourself, something you can refer back to when you need a reminder.

After Reading:
REVIEW

CONGRATULATIONS! You have now finished learning about the all of the most important ways of thinking about text *before, during,* and *after* you read. At this point, you are well on your way to becoming a strong critical reader, all it's going to take is practice and time.

By now you should understand what I meant early on in this book when I told you that practically anyone can become an expert reader. Knowing what you need to do is different than actually doing it, though. With all of the knowledge you now have about reading skills, the only thing holding you back from improving is yourself. Do not get in your own way. Keep on reading, and keep on practicing.

If you're a student, you are perfectly poised to practice these ways of thinking. When your teacher or professor asks the class a question, raise that hand! Talk to your fellow classmates. Create and meet with a study group if you haven't formed one already.

If you aren't a student, then you'll have to work a teensy bit harder to create your own community of readers, but it shouldn't be that difficult. Reach out to people you know. Send emails, texts, make some phone calls, and nab yourself a reading buddy. Join a book club! Get on the Internet, and see what other people are saying about the things you read.

Reading seems like solitary business, but it doesn't have to be. Don't make the mistake of keeping your reading to yourself.

Now, a review. Let's see how well you understand and recall what you've read so far:

- Can you name and describe all six critical reading skills and the six after reading skills?
- Which of these critical and after reading skills do you believe you have already mastered?
- Which of these critical and after reading skills do you think you will need to work on most?
- Can you name and describe all twelve before and during reading skills? Have you already incorporated most of them into your new ways of thinking as a reader?

Perhaps you should flip back through what you've read so far to make sure that your responses to these questions are accurate.

Remember: It's not enough to know these ways of thinking; you have to apply them in order to become an expert reader.

Timeout for Self-Assessment and Reflection

First of all, this calls for a celebration. You have learned a great deal about reading, and by now you have probably changed your reading ability in significant ways. Go out and grab yourself an order of celebratory cheese fries! When your fingers are licked clean, read on.

- The next three or four things you read, note how long it takes you to read them. Then, record the # of pages and your reading time. You should be reading more in less time now.

- How often do you read something and realize that you don't remember what you just read when you get to the end? Does this happen more often with certain types of readings? This should happen far less often now.

- What do you do when you find an unfamiliar word in the reading? Do you skip it? Look up the definition? Highlight it?

- Do you read *every word* in a text, or do you skip words, sentences, or paragraphs?

- If you are reading something that contains charts, pictures, or other special features, do you read them or skip over them? Say you read them, please!

- What comes to mind when you hear the word *reading?* Be honest!

- In what environment do you read? Is there noise in the background, such as music, television, or other people? Do you have your phone or a computer nearby while you read? Where are you sitting when you read? How is the light?

- How often do you find yourself distracted from a reading? Do you check text messages or Facebook while reading? Do you stop to grab a snack? Do you divide your time between the reading and any other things?

- If you are a student, how well do you do on assignments or tests based on readings that you have read? Do you do poorly even though you read the assigned readings?
- If you are a student, when do you do your assigned readings for class? Do you rush to read them at the last minute, or do you start them early enough so you won't have to rush?

Now, go back and read what you wrote the last time I asked you to do some self-reflecting. Do you see any improvements from last time? Are some things exactly the same? Consider how far you've come, and where you'd like to go moving forward, and write down the following:

- Which specific skills are working for you? Do you want to start using any of the skills even more? Do you have any other thoughts about your reading progress you'd like to note?

You should be seeing some significant improvement in your reading skills by now. If not, it's time to figure out *why*. My best guess is that you aren't truly putting these ways of thinking to work for yourself. If this is the case, do some reviewing before you move on.

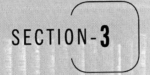

SECTION-**3**

READING FLUENCY

READING FLUENCY

Remember that fluency is one of the five components of the reading process.
Can you name all five components? Can you name the three we discuss in this book?
If not, go back to the beginning of this book to refresh your memory.

Reading fluency refers to the rate at which one reads with comprehension and expression. Think of what it means to be *fluent* in a language and apply that concept to reading. Fluent readers find it easy to read, both aloud and silently. Fluent readers understand what they're reading as they read, and they read in a way that makes it easy for listeners to understand them if they're reading aloud.

We will discuss two different kinds of reading fluency: **Oral fluency** and **silent fluency**. **Oral fluency** refers to how well people read aloud while comprehending and expressing meaning through vocal expression. **Silent fluency** refers to how well people read silently while comprehending text. **Reading rate** refers to the pace at which one reads.

Don't let this relatively short section on fluency fool you into believing that it isn't important. It's true that the comprehension skills take up the most space in this book, but practicing your reading fluency is just as important as practicing your comprehension skills. Remember, all of the reading skills are interrelated, which means that you have already improved your reading fluency by practicing your *before, during,* and *after comprehension skills.* Likewise, when you practice your fluency skills, you will improve your comprehension. Nice, isn't it?

Reading Fluency
ORAL FLUENCY

A fluent oral reader reads at a rate that is easy for both the reader and any listeners to understand. In addition, a fluent oral reader reads with **expression,** which means he expresses the meaning of what he reads through variations in his voice and his pacing.

I *always* have my reading students practice their oral fluency in class, and they *always* have the same reaction when I introduce this skill: Why do we need *this?*

I've heard the complaints: *I'm not going to be a public speaker. I never volunteer to read aloud in class. I hate reading in front of other people. What is this, middle school?*

Here's the thing: Remember that symphony of skills I discussed earlier? A symphony makes an excellent metaphor for reading because both rely on several different things happening all at once to achieve a beautiful result. The reading skills we discuss in this book are intricately interrelated, and not only that, they *need* each other.

In other words, the better you are at reading aloud, the better you will be at reading silently. The better you are at reading silently, the better your comprehension. The better your comprehension, the better your vocabulary. The better your vocabulary, the better your fluency. And . . . the better your fluency, the better you are at reading aloud, which takes us full circle. You could reverse everything I just wrote, too—the better your fluency, the better your vocabulary . . . I think you get the picture.

Also, regardless of what you choose to do in life, odds are you will find yourself in a position of being asked to read *something* aloud one day. Maybe you'll have a child one day, and you'll want to read him bedtime stories. Or an elderly loved one might need your help reading her mail. Or your boss will ask you to read a memo to everyone in a meeting. Whatever it is, when you find yourself in the position of reading aloud, you'll be grateful for the practice you're about to get.

So, in addition to developing all the ways of thinking discussed in the comprehension skills section of this book, I strongly recommend you work on your oral fluency, as well.

Improving your oral fluency is as easy as learning any other reading skill—nearly anyone can do it. It just takes practice (a lot of time) and reflection (a bit more time).

The best way to improve your oral reading skills is (wait for it . . .) to read aloud. Not much of a shock, I'm sure.

Reading Fluency
PAIRED READING FLUENCY

My favorite way to practice reading aloud is with a partner, and it's called **PAIRED FLUENCY WORK.** If you are reading this book as part of a class, then perhaps your teacher or professor will choose to incorporate **paired fluency work** into your semester. If you are reading this book on your own, I highly recommend you find a friend you trust and ask him or her to spend fifteen minutes a week reading with you.

If you aren't ready to read in front of a friend just yet, then read in front of a mirror. Whatever you do, *do not skip this section*. Start out as slowly as you'd like, but work up to reading aloud with a partner.

The paired fluency work will focus on your reading rate, comprehension, and expression while reading aloud. In addition, paired fluency work will help build your vocabulary and knowledge of text structure by exposing you to well-written passages that include unfamiliar words.

Teachers who use paired fluency in class often buy sets of reading passages to use for this work. These reading passages are assigned reading levels that usually correspond to grade levels, and the words are numbered in the passage so readers can track how many words they read per minute. Lucky for you, a quick Google search of "high school oral fluency passages" will turn up free resources for passages you can print out for your own use. At the time of publication, The Ohio Literacy Alliance has my personal favorite fluency passages available for free online at http://www.ohioliteracyalliance.org/fluency/fluency.htm.

That being said, you can use *any* text you'd like to practice your reading fluency. The advantage of texts created for oral fluency practice is that the words are numbered and they are leveled.

Read on to see how paired fluency works.

Reading Fluency
PAIRED READING FLUENCY

This is how paired fluency works:

1. Find a partner with whom you will be comfortable reading aloud

2. Print out two copies of the passage you will be reading aloud, one for each person.

3. Your partner (or teacher) should read the reading passage aloud one time while you follow along and make any notes to yourself that will help you read it aloud.

4. Now, Partner A reads the passage aloud to Partner B for one minute. (Set a timer for this. I use the count down timer at http://www.online-stopwatch.com/)

   a. As Partner A is reading aloud, Partner B follows along and marks any words that Partner A skips or misreads.

   b. At the end of one minute, Partner B puts a slash (/) behind the last word Partner A read, and write a 1 above the slash to indicate the point at which Partner A stopped reading during his first turn.

5. Now, Partner B reads the passage aloud to Partner A for one minute.

   a. As Partner B is reading aloud, Partner A follows along and marks any words that Partner B skipped or misread

   b. At the end of one minute, Partner A puts a slash (/) behind the last word Partner B read, and write a 1 above the slash to indicate the point at which Partner B stopped reading during his first turn. (You will put a 2 above the slash after your partner's second reading, and a 3 after the third reading, of course.)

6. Repeat Steps 4 and 5 until each partner has read the passage three times. Begin at the beginning of the passage each time you read.

7. Now, if you choose to, graph your progress in the fluency chart on page 139 of this book. (I recommend photocopying the page so you can always make a clean copy of the chart if you need it.)

8. Do a retell. Give yourself two or three minutes to write down everything you can remember from the passage.

9. Give yourself an **Expressive Reading** score and a **Comprehension** score using the rubrics on page 141. These scores are only for you to track your progress, so do not worry if you don't score a 5 the first time; worry only about improving over time.

Once you get used to the process, it will take you no more than 15 minutes to do your paired fluency work. This is a small time investment that reaps great rewards. I recommend practicing your oral fluency through paired fluency work at least once a week.

Reading Fluency
PAIRED READING FLUENCY

Important Notes:

- Your goal should be to read the passage smoothly and with expression. It is **NOT** a race to see who can read more words in a minute. Racing through the passage will not help you become a more fluent reader! It will just make you more difficult to understand.

- While it is not a race, over time you *will* become able to read more words per minute while maintaining your comprehension and expression. The best part about this is that it will help you become a more fluent silent reader, as well, which will then help you read *more* in *less* time. Now we are saving you time, the most precious commodity of all. (Don't say I never did anything for you).

- You and your partner should help each other become better readers. Don't be afraid to give constructive feedback. Here are the types of things you should share with each other:

  - *Pace*—Is your partner reading too quickly, too slowly, or at just the right speed to understand?

  - *Expression*—Is your partner using his voice to express the meaning of the passage? Is your partner pausing when appropriate?

  - *Details*—Is your partner skipping certain words? Mispronouncing certain words? Inserting words or replacing words?

  - *General*—How easy was it to understand your partner while she was reading?

Don't forget:

The purpose of this exercise is to improve your reading rate, comprehension, and expression together. It means very little if your reading rate is high, yet you do not understand or express any meaning while reading.

words read per minute

	1st	3rd	1st	3rd	1st	3rd	1st	3rd	1st	3rd	1st	3rd	1st	3rd	1st	3rd	1st	3rd	1st	3rd
225																				
220																				
215																				
210																				
205																				
200																				
195																				
190																				
185																				
180																				
175																				
170																				
165																				
160																				
155																				
150																				
145																				
140																				
135																				
130																				
125																				
120																				
115																				
110																				
105																				
100																				
95																				
90																				
85																				
80																				
75																				
70																				
65																				
60																				
55																				
50																				
reading	1st	3rd	1st	3rd	1st	3rd	1st	3rd	1st	3rd	1st	3rd	1st	3rd	1st	3rd	1st	3rd	1st	3rd
Expressive Score																				
Comp. Score																				
level																				
date																				

Reading Fluency
PAIRED READING FLUENCY

If you're using fluency passages, below is a sample of what they might look like. In the reading specialist world, this annotated fluency passage is called a *running record*.

The annotations I made on this running record show you the kind of notes you can take while listening to your partner read. You don't have to take such detailed notes, however. It's enough to just listen and mark words that your partner skips or reads incorrectly.

Reading Fluency
PAIRED READING FLUENCY

Reading Fluency Self-Scoring Rubrics

After completing your paired oral fluency readings, give yourself an expressive reading score and a comprehension score based using these rubrics.

Expressive Reading Rubric

Be sure to get your partner's input on your expressive score, as well.

1	2	3	4	5
Reads very slowly or very quickly. Does not pay attention to punctuation. Reads in a monotone voice (without any expression.)	Reads a little too slowly or a little too quickly. May sound choppy, with pauses or errors. Some attention is given to punctuation.	Sounds like natural language, but has some choppiness. Usually pays attention to punctuation. Errors are selfcorrected quickly and smoothly.	Reads with good expression throughout most of text. Words flow smoothly and naturally, and meaning is clear.	Reads with good expression and enthusiasm throughout the entire text. Reader varies expression to match his or her interpretation of the text.

Comprehension Self-Scoring Rubric

Use your retell to help give yourself a comprehension score.

And that's it! Remember: Practice reading aloud *at least* once a week.

1	2	3	4	5
No recall or minimal recall of only a fact or two from the passage.	Student can recall a number of unrelated facts of varied importance.	Student can recall the main idea of the passage with a few supporting details.	Student can recall the main idea with a large amount of supporting details, although they may not be organized as presented in the passage.	Student can recall the main idea with supporting details in logical order, and can make connections beyond the text to his or her own personal life, to another text, etc.

Reading Fluency
SILENT READING FLUENCY

A fluent silent reader reads at a rate and with expression that supports his own comprehension.

You may be wondering how you read with expression while reading silently. Remember when we discussed the voice in your head back when I introduced *metacognition* as a during reading skill? Well, *that* is the voice that needs to read with expression while you read silently. It took me a few years of teaching reading before I figured this out, but I was shocked to learn that many of my students used a boring, monotone voice to read to themselves during silent reading.

Unless you are a librarian or primary school teacher, most of the reading you will do in life is going to be done in silence and on your own. Therefore, your silent reading fluency skills are extremely important for your success as a reader. It also doesn't hurt that the more fluently you read, the faster you can read, and therefore the *more books* you can read. Or, at the very least, it will take you less time to complete your homework or other obligatory reading. Not too shabby.

As for practicing your silent fluency, you've been doing that since you started reading this book! As you know, the work you're doing to improve all of your other reading skills will help you become a more fluent silent reader, and vice versa. Isn't that wonderful?

I don't have a series of silent fluency skills for you to learn and practice, although I do have some tips. Of course I have more to say on this subject. Did you expect any less?

Reading Fluency
SILENT READING FLUENCY

Silent Reading Fluency Tip #1: Find Your Reading Zone

One thing that seriously affects your success as a silent reader is the quality of your **reading zone.** Remember when I discussed this in the Introduction?

Have you ever heard anyone say they were *in the zone*? Sometimes we hear athletes say they were in the zone during the game, or artists say they are in the zone while creating. The zone is that state where you become so focused on something that the rest of the word slips away and your entire being is focused on your one task. Lately, psychologists who study this phenomenon have been calling this *being in flow.* Whatever you call it, *one of the most effective things you can do to help yourself as a reader is to identify your reading zone.*

Think of something that you love to do. Perhaps it's cooking, or bobsledding, or making jewelry out of dried macaroni pasta. Have you ever slipped into the zone while doing your thing? That's what I mean.

Your reading zone is the atmosphere in which you do your best reading. It is the place that is most likely to help you get into the zone when you read. When you sit down to read, you *must* make sure that you're putting yourself in an environment that is going to help you do your best reading.

I can't tell you what your reading zone is, because that's something that only you can identify. I *can* tell you about my reading zone, though:

- I do my best reading on a big, squashy dark brown sofa in my living room,
- with a warm blanket over my legs, and
- a floor lamp with yellow light turned on, and
- a big mug of something hot by my side—coffee or hot cocoa, and
- either no sound at all, OR music without words or music that I don't know very well (so I'm not tempted to sing along), and
- a dog or cat (or both) curled up with me.

There are also things I absolutely cannot have around while reading because they are too distracting:

- I can't eat while reading because it slows me down. Weird as it is, I start to read one word every time I chew . . . which . . . is . . . a . . . very . . . slow . . . process.
- No music with words that I know, because I will start to sing along and ignore my reading.
- I hide all technology (cell phone and laptop) so I'm not tempted to check texts or websites.
- No televisions on while I'm reading, that is too distracting.

Over the next few weeks, pay attention to the things that help you get in the zone, and more importantly, the things that distract you while reading and pull you out of the zone. Once you understand what you need to do your best reading, work on creating your reading zone.

Don't be afraid to venture out of your home to find places that could become your reading zone. When I was an undergraduate student I found two places that helped me do my best reading. One was in the library on the engineering quad. I was an English major and therefore couldn't even get access to the computers in that library, but that place was *perfect* for studying, for me at least. It was filled with these huge, dark, heavy wooden tables and matching chairs. If you didn't know to lift the chair up when you pulled it out it made this gigantic screech that echoed through the entire place, so everyone would look up at you and know you were a newbie to the library. Otherwise, the place was silent, so I went there when I really needed to focus or catch up on something.

My other reading spot in undergrad was in the vending room of the student union. This place was nearly the opposite of the engineering library—the tables were rickety, the people were loud, and there was the hum from the vending machines and the regular sound of food and cans crashing down. It was perfect. This is where my study group met every night. We'd work silently for a while on our individual reading, then someone would grab a bag of microwave popcorn, and we'd take a study break together.

Which reminds me: You may have different reading zones that work best for different purposes. Whatever they are, find them, and claim them. Bonus points if you form a study group, too.

Reading Fluency
SILENT READING FLUENCY

Silent Reading Fluency Tip #2: Vary Your Reading Rate

Reading rate refers to the pace at which one reads. Most people are in the habit of reading everything at one speed, but this is *not* ideal. Varying reading rate can save time and improve comprehension.

This is another one of those things I only realized after working with students in reading classes for several years—that some struggling readers read everything at the same pace. Paying attention to your reading rate is a tiny thing that can help comprehension in big ways.

You *should* read more slowly when the material is difficult, or when you're seeking high comprehension. Alternatively, you should read faster when the material is easy or when you're skimming for information.

Think of the way you vary your speech depending on the situation. My guess is that you speak to your teachers or professors differently than you speak to your closest friends. And what about the way you would speak to an elderly person who has a difficult time hearing—would you slow down and enunciate? Probably. Reading is similar; different situations require different reading rates.

Just for fun, here are some numbers about reading rates. Notice that difficult material takes skilled readers longer to read than easy material.

Reading Rates of Skilled Readers*

	Difficult Material	Easy Material	Skimming
Speed	200 – 300 WPM	250 – 500 WPM	800 + WPM
Comprehension	80 – 90%	70%	50%

*from Locating and Correcting Reading Difficulties *by Shanker and Ekwall*

Start paying attention to your reading rate when you sit down to read various texts. If you're boring yourself by reading too slowly, speed it up! If you are missing important information, on the other hand, consider slowing it down.

Reading Fluency
SILENT READING FLUENCY

Silent Reading Fluency Tip #3: Don't Bore Yourself

I already mentioned this earlier, but many struggling readers use boring, monotone voices when reading to themselves. This is something I was shocked to learn, because I just couldn't understand why anyone would do that to herself!

Now, I'm not saying you need to go over the top and exaggerate every word you read as if you were a kindergarten teacher reading a story to a bunch of adorable kids. But what you should do is use expression while reading silently. This seems like a small thing, but this change alone can greatly improve your comprehension, and it will *definitely* help you stay focused on the reading.

Reading Fluency
SILENT READING FLUENCY

Silent Reading Fluency Tip #4: Skimming and Scanning

Skimming is the act of reading material rapidly and superficially. Skimming requires less comprehension than normal reading and can be an effective way to preview material before you read it more closely.

Check your own ability to skim by picking up a new piece of reading material and looking it over very quickly—are you able to determine the general gist of the material by skimming through it?

You can use skimming to find the idea of what an article or book is about before you buy or print it, to preview a chapter in a textbook, or to see if a particular website might have the information you are looking for on a search.

Skimming *is not* an adequate replacement for actually reading something that you should be reading start to finish. Instead, think of it as a tool for assessing a text *before* you read. The things you do while practicing your before reading skills all rely on skimming to an extent, so this is likely a skill you have already practiced.

Scanning is the act of searching for specific information or the answers to specific questions about material by reading it quickly. Scanning is faster than skimming, and it requires even less comprehension.

Check your own ability to scan by searching for a number of specific facts or terms in a textbook chapter. If you are unable to do this in a reasonable time limit, you may have difficulties scanning.

You scan when you search for a particular class in a course schedule, for example. If you want to find the times for Professor Ladeedah's English 101 class, you aren't going to open up the course schedule to page 1 and start reading there. Instead, you'll flip to the English section and scan the class list until Ladeedah's name pops out at you. Scanning is an important skill because without it you'd be forced to read through a lot of unnecessary text.

How do readers improve their skimming and scanning abilities?

These are skills that will develop over the normal course of your reading experiences. Whenever you *need* to skim or scan material, you will have the opportunity to practice the skill.

VOCABULARY

Vocabulary
VOCABULARY INTRODUCTION

Now we come to vocabulary—the third prong of our approach to developing reading ability in this book. (Just a reminder: the first two prongs are comprehension and fluency. Together, vocabulary, comprehension and fluency make up three of the five components of the reading process. Can you remember what the other two components are?)

It is a fact that there is a strong relationship between vocabulary knowledge and comprehension. This means that the stronger a person's vocabulary, the stronger their ability to comprehend what they read. In addition, the oral language practice and the act of reading itself are two vital methods for increasing vocabulary. **In other words,** the more you speak and listen to others speak and the more you read about a variety of subjects, the more you will increase your vocabulary.

Another fact that may interest you is this: specific vocabulary instruction, or the use of the dictionary to learn new words, only account for a very small percentage of the way adults learn new vocabulary. *What does this mean?* This means that memorizing vocabulary lists is not a particularly useful activity.

Instead, to increase your vocabulary, you must do the following:
- Read. Often.
- Speak and listen.
- Read some more.
- Build a depth and breadth of meaning for the words

you use and encounter (in other words—build an understanding beyond the dictionary definition)
- Develop an interest in words
- Relate words to your own life
- Develop the ability to learn new words independently
- Identify and examine unfamiliar words that you encounter while listening and reading.

An Important Note on Word Learning

When learning vocabulary, think in terms of *concepts* and *labels* rather than just *definitions*. We often understand the core concept (e.g. "car") of something, but we are not yet aware of the labels (e.g. "brake pad") that are associated with the thing. When you learn new words, consider whether they fit under a concept that you already know, and *then* learning the new word will become easier for you.

Vocabulary
JUICY WORDS

Become an Arbiter of Lexical Style

We know expert readers develop their vocabulary by exposure to new words through reading and listening, but *how* do they do it, exactly?

The answer is this: They keep track of those new words, they learn their meaning, and they incorporate them into their own usage. In other words, once an expert reader runs into a new word in a newspaper or book, she writes it down, looks up the meaning, and makes note of it. She may refer back to the word and its meaning again then try to use it herself. Once she uses it herself—voila! She has just added another word to her vocabulary.

I call these unfamiliar words I encounter *juicy words*. They're juicy because they're exciting; they add a new dimension to my ability to express and communicate. I've been keeping lists of juicy words for years and years, and that is the primary way that I have developed my own vocabulary.
Now, it's your turn.

You are going to become a *collector of juicy words*. Any time you encounter an unfamiliar word, write it down. You will encounter juicy words while reading, of course, but also while listening—to lectures, the radio, conversations with friends. The source doesn't matter, what matters is that you start developing the habit of identifying unfamiliar words when you encounter them, and then writing them down.

I recommend you keep your juicy words list where you'll be able to access it easily. I have an app on my phone that lets me take quick notes, so I keep my juicy words list there.

Start collecting unfamiliar words *right now.* The next word you encounter that is unfamiliar, write it down!

However, it is not enough to just collect juicy words . . . You must use them!

Knowing and doing are two different things, after all, right? Start out by challenging yourself to use a small amount of juicy words every week, say just two or three. You can use them in your speech or in your writing. Pick the words you plan to use and think about ways you might be able to use them, and then just wait—an opportunity will present itself.

This will soon become habit, and you won't have to remind yourself to collect and use juicy words anymore. All it takes is time and practice. Sounds familiar, right?

Vocabulary
WORD PARTS

The English language has its roots in several languages, primarily Greek and Latin. This means that there are common roots and affixes (prefixes and suffixes) that appear in multiple words in the language.

Example of a Word Root:

PAC/PEAS is related to the Latin words for "agree" and "peace." The Pacific Ocean—that is, the "Peaceful Ocean"—was named by Magellan because it seemed so calm after the storms near Cape Horn. (He obviously never witnessed a Pacific hurricane.)

This example is taken from English Words from Latin and Greek Elements *by Donald Ayers.*

Example of a Prefix:

a-/an means "not" or "without." Examples: apolitical, atheist, anonymous

Example of a Suffix:

-age is a noun which means "activity," or "result of action." Examples: courage, suffrage, shrinkage
By studying the most common roots and affixes, you will increase your ability to make an educated guess about the meaning of unfamiliar words that contain these word parts. This is an effective way to study words because learning just one word root will actually help you identify the meaning of many words.

How do I start?

There are several ways to do this. The easiest is to take a look at your juicy words list and look for roots and affixes among the words. Once you find a root in a word, for example, look at the word's meaning and take a guess at what the root might mean. Then brainstorm a list of other words that contain the same root and see if all of the words have a common thread of meaning among them. Chances are they will! Double-check the meaning with a reference source, and relish your newfound word knowledge!

A more systematic way of learning would be to identify a root or affix and brainstorm as many words as you can that contain the word part. Then look for a common thread of meaning among all the words, give a guess as to the word part's meaning, and then double-check your guess with a reference source. Choose a specific number of affixes to add to your word knowledge every week, and you will be on your way to building your vocabulary.

Vocabulary
COMMONLY CONFUSED WORDS

The final component of our vocabulary study is commonly confused words. These words are commonly confused for a variety of reasons but mostly because they either look or sound alike.

I like the commonly confused words that are listed on The University of Richmond's Writing Center website at http://writing2.richmond.edu/writing/wweb/conford.html.

Take a look at the site and get into the habit of identifying words that you commonly confuse in your own writing. When (if) you write essays, which words are most often identified when you run a spell check? Which words do you always confuse with one another?

Pay attention to these words, and develop little tools for helping yourself remember the difference between them. Here's an example of a simple device that we often learn in elementary school:

Desert vs. Dessert
Dessert with the extra s refers to the sweet treat we eat at the end of the meal. We add an extra s because we always want an extra piece of dessert!

This is a really simple trick to remembering the difference, and often this is all that it takes.

Try to develop your own tricks for distinguishing between commonly confused words. Bonus points if you write them down.

There are many great comics available on the Internet that cleverly distinguish between commonly confused and mistaken words. Two worth checking out are:

The Oatmeal's Grammar Comics: http://theoatmeal.com/tag/grammar

Hyperbole and a Half's blog post "The Alot is Better than You at Everything"

http://hyperboleandahalf.blogspot.com/2010/04/alot-is-better-than-you-at-everything.html

These are hilarious and borderline inappropriate: the perfect combination to make the information extremely memorable.

Vocabulary
A FINAL WORD ON WORDS

There is one other thing to keep in mind while reading.

Don't assume you know better than the writer.
This is another one of those things I only realized many people do after working with struggling readers for several years: when they come to a word that is familiar but *seems* to be used incorrectly, some readers assume that it's an error on the writer's part. Likewise, when they come across a word that looks like a word they know with only a small difference, they assume it is an editing error.

While it could be an error, it could also be that the word is being used in a way that is unfamiliar to you. If you assume a word is used in error and you just move on that means two things: One, you are going to miss out on some of the author's meaning because, two, you just missed an opportunity to expand your word knowledge, so you will remain incorrect in your understanding of the particular word in question.

Here's an example of this from my own reading experience (italics are mine):

"The interior of the bus was a *fug* of blue-gray smoke." I recently read this line in Stephen King's excellent book, *11/22/63*. I read this book on my Kindle, so my first assumption was that this was an error in the translation from the print copy to the Kindle version of the book, and so I assumed the word should be *fog* instead of *fug*.

Just to be sure I did a quick search and learned that *fug* means "A heavy, stale atmosphere, especially the musty air of an overcrowded or poorly ventilated room." (thefreedictionary.com) I was *this close* to making the very mistake I'm warning you against right now, and had I made that mistake I would have continued on in ignorance about what the word *fug* means.

Don't let this be you. Never assume that you found an error in the writing, and instead **always** assume that you have just stumbled on an opportunity to learn something new about a word.

When you find these things that appear to be errors, do a quick check. Search for the word in your favorite dictionary, and if it turns out that you just discovered a new way to use it, add it to your list of juicy words! (I recommend Merriam Webster's online dictionary, http://www.merriam-webster.com/)

SECTION-**5**

APPLYING YOUR READING
SKILLS

Applying Your Reading Skills
INTRODUCTION

Okay, now it's game time. All of the work you've done so far—the comprehension skills building, the fluency practice, the word study—it's all been *practice* for the real purpose of reading, and that is to *apply what you read*. If this was a sport, applying your reading is the game. After all, what good is it to read and understand something if you don't do anything with it? (Just about as useful as a million dollars that you cannot spend.)

The most common method of applying your reading is going to come in the form of writing. After all—reading and writing are reciprocal skills, so the better you read, the better you'll write, and vice versa.

THINKING LIKE A WRITER

Now it's time to switch sides—you've been working on thinking like a reader for all this time, now you get to think like a writer.

When you write about your reading, there are four main things to keep in mind:

Audience—For whom are you writing?
Purpose—Why are you writing?
Speed—Is this detail worth slowing down and really describing, or is this the time to speed up and summarize?
Focus—Does your writing have a strong focus? Are the ideas logically connected, and do you use specific details when necessary?

WRITING AS A READER

We are going to discuss three different types of writing as a reader:

> **Summaries**—Put the main idea of the reading into your own words, and include only the main points.
>
> Responses—Discuss an *original idea* that you had in response to the reading.
>
> **Critiques**—Critically discuss an element of the reading, such as its validity, tone, effectiveness, or whether it serves its intended purpose or audience.

Applying Your Reading Skills
WRITING SUMMARIES

A **summary** is a brief restatement, *in your own words*, of the author's main idea or ideas. A summary should also include the supporting details that the author used to support her main idea. **Summaries do not include personal responses, positive or negative.**

Why is it useful for readers to write summaries? Good question! Writing summaries is a great way to assess your own comprehension of the reading material. Also, the process of writing a summary helps you reflect on the information and internalize it so it will stay with you longer.

Summaries should:
- Be about 15% to 25% as long as the original piece (excluding novels, of course)
- Identify the author, title, and source of the reading
- Identify the writer's main point(s)
- Identify the most important supporting points or details
- Identify *how* the writer makes these points (e.g. tells a story, describes a situation, provides statistics, etc.)
- Make clear the relationship between the main point and the supporting points.
- Condense these points without omitting important ideas.
- Use your own words!

- **Not** include your own observations, evaluations, or interpretations; focus only on the author's ideas and feelings. (Save your feelings for your reading responses.)

Summary Suggestion

Pack a lot of information into your first sentence including the author and title of the piece that you are summarizing.

Examples:

In her essay "Nature's Awesome Beauty," Meno Miyake discusses how a trip to the wilderness of Alaska changed her views and perspectives about nature.

In her essay, "Class of 2001," Rosa Garcia highlights important moments in her high school career by describing the thoughts and memories that go through her head as she takes part in her high school graduation.

In her essay "Growing Up in Cabrini Green," Genette Lee describes her experiences moving into and living in the projects from age eight until her senior year of high school and explores the effects this experience has had on her.

* Much of this information on writing summaries was provided by Ms. Jennifer Staben, writing professor extraordinaire, at the College of Lake County in Grayslake, Illinois.

Applying Your Reading Skills
WRITING READING RESPONSES

A **reading response** is a personal response to a reading. Reading responses focus on an original idea you had in response to reading the text.

Why is useful for readers to write reading responses? Reading responses are a wonderful way to connect with the reading, and as you know—the more you connect with what you read, the better you will comprehend it. In addition, writing reading responses encourages you dig a bit deeper into the reading to understand it even more. Writing reading responses also encourages you to see how the reading is relevant to your own life, which *really* increases your understanding. And finally, it helps you retain the information you read.

If, before you begin reading, you know you will be required to write a reading response to a particular text, be sure to pay extra attention to the voice in your head. Your best original ideas will be found there. This is also a good reason to *always* take notes of your thoughts while reading, as you never know when you'll be asked to discuss a text.

Responses should:

- Identify the author, title, and source of the reading
- Focus on one *original idea* that you had in response to the reading
- Make clear why this idea is relevant (or should be relevant) to the reader
- Make clear how your idea connects to the reading
- Use your own words!
- Include your own observations, evaluations, or interpretations, and compare them to the author's.

Applying Your Reading Skills
WRITING CRITIQUES

A **critique** critically discusses an element of the reading, such as its validity, tone, effectiveness, or whether it serves its intended purpose or audience.

Why is it useful for readers to write critiques? A critique is an in-depth analysis of the reading, and thus it requires the reader to critically examine and respond to the reading. This is an excellent way to develop your in-depth knowledge of a particular subject, or viewpoint. Your ability to write a sound critique is also a good indication of how well you understand the reading and how its subject fits into a larger context.

Critiques should:
- Identify the author, title, and source of the reading
- Focus on one aspect of the reading, such as validity, tone, effectiveness, bias, etc.
- Provide clear and valid support for your claims

Applying Your Reading Skills
TAKING A READING TEST

It may be unavoidable. One day, you may have to take a test that measures your reading ability. Here are some things to keep in mind as you prepare to take a reading test.

Preparing for the Test

- *Scope it out before you take it.* What is the format of the test? What type of questions will it ask? Is it timed? Where will you be taking it? How long is it? Is it computerized? The more you know about the test before you sit down to take it, the more comfortable you will feel on test day.

- *Get some sleep.* You will be able to focus better and recall what you have learned about reading better after a good night's sleep.

- *Eat a good breakfast.* You've heard this so many times it probably sounds like background noise, but the last thing you need on test day is to be distracted by hunger pangs. The more comfortable you are, the easier it will be to concentrate on the test, and the better you concentrate, the better you will perform.

Taking the Test

- *If you get nervous, breathe.* Don't let your nerves break your concentration and your ability to perform your best. If you find yourself getting nervous or worked up while taking the test, stop, take a breather, and give yourself time to relax before you move on.

- *Take your time.* Don't rush through questions. Make sure that you fully understand the instructions and that you read each item well enough to know *exactly* what you're answering.
- *Check your work.* If you finish before your time is up, go back and recheck your work. I know you will probably be eager to turn that test in and never see it again, but don't cave in to this desire—don't ruin your score by rushing through the test and failing to double-check your work in the end.
- *Be positive.* You have worked really hard, so now it's time to show off the fruits of your efforts.

The Most Common Types of Test Questions

You have already learned how to identify all of the information you could possibly be asked to identify on a reading test because you've already gone through all of the BDA (before-during-after) reading strategies in this packet. Hooray! Here are some examples of questions that ask you to identify:

The Main Idea
- Which of the following best states the main idea of the passage?
- The best title for this passage would be
- What is the theme of this passage?

Details
- According to the author
- The passage states that
- All of the following are false except

Inferences
- The author feels
- It can be inferred that
- The author suggests

The Author's Purpose
- The author wrote this to
- The primary purpose of this passage is
- The author is trying to

Vocabulary
- As used in this passage, the word (insert word here) means
- The best definition of (insert word here) is

SECTION-**6**

READING JUST BECAUSE

Applying Your Reading Skills
READING, JUST BECAUSE

If you take only one thing away from this book, I hope it's this: **reading can be enjoyable.** Or useful. Or interesting, intriguing, inspiring, life changing—you fill in the blank.

The point is that there are many purposes for reading, and they extend far beyond reading for a class or for work. I've already shared that reading has been and continues to be one of the greatest joys in my life, and my hope for you is that you experience even one sliver of the joy I get from reading.

> Just to give you some ideas, here's a snapshot of the kind of reading I do on a regular basis:
> - Sunday mornings with *The New York Times*. This is my favorite time of the entire week! If it's nice outside I sit out on the back deck with hot coffee, breakfast, the paper, and my dogs. If it's cold outside, I curl up in my reading chair and read the paper, starting with the Book Review.
> - **Book Club.** I'm in a wonderful book club with wonderful women. We read one book a month, then everyone comes together on a Friday night. We eat a meal together and laugh and argue and discuss what we read for hours and hours. We read fiction and nonfiction and everything in between.
> - **Lazy afternoons with my magazines.** I subscribe to a couple of magazines and I save them up and read them on days when I have some free time on my hands.

- **Rereading my favorites.** I reread a handful of books throughout the year because I love them so much, going back and reading them again is like seeing an old friend after being apart for a long time. I carry a book with me everywhere I go, and I love to find new places to read—coffee shops, bookstores, outdoor parks, etc.
- **Developing new skills and experiences.** I love to learn new things, and whenever something new piques my interest I do some reading about it before I dive in. I've recently become interesting in making wooden toys, for example, so I found a great book about beginning woodworking and took it out of the library. It's amazing what you can accomplish once you realize that the resources are all available to you.
- **Keeping in touch.** I keep in touch with friends and family on a daily basis by reading their posts on Facebook, sending text messages and emails, and yes—even sending handwritten notes. (I wish more people wrote handwritten notes, but that's a topic for another book.)

There are so many joys to be had with reading. Yours may be very different than mine, but whatever they are, my wish for you is that you discover them.

Book Club
INTRODUCTION

What happens in Book Club, stays in Book Club.

What is this all about?

I bet that most of you have never experienced the thrill of being in a book club, so I am excited to introduce you to this wonderful experience.

A book club is typically a group of people who voluntarily get together, choose an interesting book to read, read the book on their own, then come together once again to discuss what the book meant to them, why they did or did not like it, and how it changed something about the way they think, feel, believe, or look at the world. Book club meetings usually have a lot of food and great conversation, as well, and they usually take place in someone's home. A typical book club meeting lasts anywhere from two to five hours.

If you're reading this book for a class, then I strongly encourage your instructor to host a class book club. If you're reading this book on your own, then I strongly encourage you to create a book club. Your book club experience will be different from a typical classroom or work-related reading experience because the *purpose* for reading will be different. Typically, when you read a novel for a class your purpose is to remember details of the novel, to perform well on periodic reading quizzes, to study the text for literary devices and form, and to write some sort of essay about the book. As a book club member, your purpose is to enjoy the book, to let it change you in some way, and to share an enjoyable reading experience with a group of people so you can all learn something from each other.

Why advocate for instructors to host book clubs in class, you ask? The answer is simple: Book club is the best way I know to help students experience the joy of reading. Also, it doesn't hurt that I also know that when you enjoy reading a book, it makes you a better reader. But overall, I just want you to have some fun.

Book Club
HOW IT WORKS

Class book clubs usually work like this:

First, every student will bring in a book they'd like to read on an assigned day, then one by one they'll pitch the book to the class. After all the books have been shared, students will have time to form book clubs of four to six people who want to read the same book. Over the years I've learned that four to six members in a book club is the magic size.

Second, the newly formed book clubs will sit down together, introduce themselves, and take a look at the book they've just committed to read. Everyone should get their hands on a copy of the book as soon as possible.

Third, you read! I require my students to read no fewer than 50 pages per week. My student book clubs create their reading schedule together and give me a copy so I can read along with them.

Finally, book club meetings! I have my student book clubs meet every other week in class. In addition to reading the book, every student chooses a role and brings in a set of ten book club contributions, which I will explain in the next section. Everyone also brings in some food to share. I've found that food makes everything so much more fun. During the actual book club meeting, the book clubs sit together, eat together, and discuss their books. I usually hang out in the classroom but out of the way and let my students do their thing.

Now, I know that you may be thinking book club is for older women who like to knit and drink tea, at least, for some reason this is the image my students most often tell me they have of book club ladies. But this is simply not true. I started my own book club when I was 28, I can't knit, and I'm a coffee gal. Seriously, though—my students often cite book club as their favorite part of my reading classes. It is a wonderful way to make real connections with people, and it is the best way I know how to help people become better readers.

Book Club
CONTRIBUTIONS

Book Club Contributions

As a member of Book Club you have two obligations: to enjoy reading your book, and to contribute to your book club meetings. In order to ensure the success of your book club, each member will be responsible for choosing a book club role, and for bringing in contributions based on that role for each book club discussion. (Everyone also brings food to share to Book Club so we can eat together while we discuss our books.)

The Book Club Roles:

- **Discussion Leader.** The Discussion Leader is responsible for leading the book club discussion and ensuring that it stays alive and on course. Discussion leaders contribute *at least five* discussion questions about the section of the book read for the meeting. Their remaining five contributions can be anything at all, they do not have to be discussion questions.
    - Please note that discussion questions are questions that *do not* have a simple answer, so no "yes" or "no" questions, and no questions that have a right or wrong answer, or can be answered in just a short sentence. (Such questions are quiz questions, not discussion questions.) Rather, discussion questions are intriguing; they inspire people to think for themselves and to provide original, personal ideas when they answer.
- **Predictor.** Predictors are responsible for identifying and sharing *at least five predictions* about what will happen

in the upcoming sections of the book. (So, this means that you won't have a Predictor for the last meeting of book club, since you will have finished the book.) Their remaining five contributions can be anything at all, they do not have to be predictions. Predictors should include the "clues" and page numbers where they can be found when recording their predictions for book club.

- **Connector.** The Connector is responsible for identifying and sharing *at least five parts of the book where he or she can make a connection to the story.* These connections may be personal, or they may be connections to other people, stories, movies, or things you have encountered. Connectors should record the actual lines from the book and the page numbers where they found the connections, as well as a brief description of the connection to each section. Their remaining five contributions can be anything at all, they do not have to be connections.

- **Journalist.** Journalists are responsible for identifying and sharing *at least five key moments in the reading.* Just as a good journalist knows to report only on the most interesting or crucial points in a story, the Journalist's job is to identify the key moments in the reading. Don't forget to include page #s along with a brief description of why you believe this to be a key moment in the story. Their remaining five contributions can be anything at all, they do not have to be key points.

Contribution work should be easy and low-pressure. The purpose of the contributions is really twofold. One, they help keep everyone on track while reading independently, and two, they help get the ball rolling during the first book club meetings.

It doesn't hurt that seeing others' contributions will also give you insight into the different ways that the same story can be viewed by different people. I include several pages of actual contributions that students have shared in my class Book Clubs. Take a look at these sample contributions to see the different impressions books have made on my students, and pay attention to how personal their reactions are to the books they read.

Book Club
SAMPLE CONTRIBUTIONS

Here are some great contributions from actual students in my classes. Please use these as inspiration as you create your own contributions for Book Club.

Discussion Leader

- What does it show on the parents' behalf that they are willing to move to this new house in Phoenix, Arizona that is infested with roaches, neighbors who are gypsies and steal, a neighborhood known for having sexual predators, and Brian having a hatchet? What can you tell about the parents and their character already so early on in the book? – K. B. (*The Glass Castle*)
- Do you think Rex switching jobs so often takes a toll on the children? If so, how? – K. B. (*The Glass Castle*)
- We know that Rex gets mad easily. What triggers you to get mad? – K. B. (*The Glass Castle*)
- She started straightening her hair and dressing differently. Why do you think her parents hated her new "hippie look"? What do looks have to do with personality? – M. M. (*Go Ask Alice*)
- Throughout all these years do you really think all that history could have been lost? – K. S. (*The Lost Symbol*)
- Why do you think it is important to the story that Tita was born in the kitchen? – H. K. (*Like Water for Chocolate*)
- What do you think Cisneros meant when she said

"his scrutiny changed their relationship forever?"
– R. E. *(Like Water for Chocolate)*

- What kinds of things do you do with your family or friends that are similar to how Ben, Callie, and Antonia pretend to be pirates? – M. C. (*The Weight of Silence*)
- Do you still feel shame about something you've done years ago? Would you like to share? (pg. 144) – M. V. (*The Weight of Silence*)
- The author of the book, Adeline Yen Mah, begins the story with her father's will. What do you think is the purpose for starting it this way? – A. C. (*Falling Leaves*)
- In the early 1900s there were arranged marriages in China. What would you do if you were in that situation? – A. C. (*Falling Leaves*)
- Why do you think Delia was expecting her death to come after she saw the rose? – C. M. *(V for Vendetta)*
- Why is it so important to feel good? (p. 35) – M. I. *(The Secret)*
- The author of the book, Rhonda Byrne, begins her story by telling how everything was terrible in her life. For such a positive book like *The Power* it is a very interesting way to start a discussion. What do you think is her purpose for starting it this way? (p. ix) – A. K. *(The Power)*
- Do you think it is possible to always think positive? Do you think people can really control their thoughts? (p. 16) – A. K. *(The Power)*

Predictor

The Glass Castle
- In the beginning of the book Janette states that she sees her mom by a dumpster, so by this I know that the mom and dad will remain outcasts throughout the entire story. – L. M.

Three Cups of Tea
- As he was on the mountain freezing, he starts to think about his sister and how he helped her be more independent and how she suddenly died. He was going to leave her necklace at the top of K2 in her honor. I predict that he will talk about his sister's life and how it was different after she had gotten sick. – K. G.

The Weight of Silence
- Peter and Calli's disappearances have some similarities to the first girl who is still missing, so I think that the two cases have a connection to each other, and suspect that they might be the same person. – C. R.

Connector

Like Water for Chocolate
- On one of our Indian TV shows there is a father with four daughters. The youngest daughter has to take care of her father just like Tita has to care for her mother in the book. (pg. 11) – N. P.

Go Ask Alice

- "I will be a positively different person by the time we get to our new home." (pg. 4) When I was going into high school I thought exactly how she did. I was going to be a completely different person, and thinking if I were to be how people would want me to be, then it would be easier for me to fit in. – G. M.
- "I'm partly somebody else trying to fit in and say the right things and do the right things and be in the right place and wear what everybody else is wearing." (pg. 11) I don't always feel like I am myself because I try to be what people want me to be so I can fit in. I am not perfect and no one is, but I do try hard to fit in. – G. M.

V for Vendetta

- The "Leader" in this book reminds me of the Kingpin from the cartoon *Spiderman* because they are both big men with a lot of power, and people that work for them are somewhat like henchmen. – R. R.
- This book also has the same kind of theme as *Spiderman* because they are both very dark, they are both vigilantes for a purpose, and they also both lost their parents when they were young. – R. R.

Three Cups of Tea

- One part of the book talked about the Duke of Abruzzi being stunned by the stark beautify of the encircling peak, and how nothing could compare to this in terms of alpine beauty. The way I connect to this fact of the book is when I visited Yosemite National Park I saw that it covers huge parts of the Western Sierra Nevada in central

California and has innumerable lakes, meadows, forest, and a granite summit with endless, unspoiled alpine scenery. (p. 8) – Z. B.

Journalist

V for Vendetta
- The first key moment in the book would be when "V" makes his appearance for the first time because he is the main character in the novel. He is the one that makes the story as great as it is due to his mysteriousness. Our curiosity for finding out his true identity is what hooks us on to the book. (pg. 10) – C. M.
- Kidnapping The Voice of Faith becomes the fourth imperative moment. The Voice of Faith, who also goes by the name of Lewis, is the person who shoves all the dictator's ideas into people's minds every single day. This shows that "V" has a strategy for everything he does, regardless of if it is illegal or not. Also, by not having someone to imprint the dictator's beliefs in the nation's mind, the dictator became weaker and "V" can now make his point and prove to everyone how dishonored their government is. (pg. 20) – C. M.

Go Ask Alice
- "Yesterday I bought this diary because I thought I would have something wonderful and great to say." (pg. 1) I thought this was important because if she had never bought this diary then this book would have never been written. – B. F.
- "I wonder if I could go stick my finger down my throat and throw up after every meal." (pg. 10)

This is a critical point because this shows that she could hurt herself. – C. M.

- "I'd better take some of Gramp's sleeping pills, I'm never going to be able to sleep without them." This is a key point because it shows how she got to a stage where the only way she could be relaxed and sleep is by taking pills. She just stepped into a really bad addiction where she needs professional help. – C. M.

- Throughout the book she was harassed by the kids in school. I believe this played a huge role in her death because she might have killed herself because she was stressed out, or maybe she was trying to get high so she could forget about them. We will never know. – A. I.

The Lost Symbol

- "The ancient marked their bodies with ink as a way of offering their bodies in partial sacrifice." (pg. 10) I think this is a key moment because it shows that some people will do anything to live. – K. S.

The Weight of Silence

- There is nothing physically wrong with Calli, but still she urinates and does not talk. This is the first key fact I found because it shows us that there is a secret that hides behind her being speechless. (pg. 14) - M. L.

Falling Leaves

- Adeline's great aunt refuses to have her feet bound, making them ache and smell. (pg. 5) I think that her great aunt rejecting foot binding at the young age of three is symbolic that she is a strong person and very independent, and she shows that later on throughout her life. – G. P.

The Glass Castle

- The beginning of the mistreatment from Aunt Erma to the children (from hitting them in the head with a spoon to keeping them in the basement, to starting a physical fight with Lori) is an important aspect of the novel. This is crucial because Aunt Erma is taking advantage while the parents are away from the children and they have no one to stand by their side. (pg. 146) – L. M.

Book Club
CHOOSING YOUR BOOK

If you're participating in a book club for a class, I recommend that your instructor assign a Book Club Pitch, which is where everyone in the class takes a couple minutes to "pitch" their book to the class. A Book Club Pitch will be your chance to advertise your book choice to your class to try to win people over to join your book club. But whether you are forming a book club on your own, or participating in a class book club, these tips will help everyone who is looking for a book to read with a group.

Looking for a book to choose for your Book Club?

Here are a few suggestions to help you find a good book:

Get thee on Goodreads.com!
- If you have ever enjoyed reading a book, look it up on Goodreads and then check out the people who have given it five stars. Go through their bookshelves to find other books they've liked. Chances are you might like those books, too.

Spend some time in an actual bookstore!
- Browse in the fiction section.
- Pick up random books and see if you like them.
- Ask employees for recommendations—chances are, they've read a lot of books, and they'll be able to help you out.

- Libraries are great, too, and I definitely love my library. However, there's something exciting about the shiny new books on bookstore shelves. I always recommend that my students *find* the book they want to read at the bookstore, then go check it out from their library.

Ask your friends.
- Have any readers in your life? Ask them for recommendations. Maybe they'll even have a copy of the book, and you can borrow it for Book Club.

Remember—*You* choose your own Book Club books, so finding something you are going to enjoy reading is the top priority. I highly recommend you put some thought into the books you pitch for Book Club. An enthusiastic, knowledgeable pitch is far more likely to make it into a Book Club than one made by someone who clearly doesn't know much about the book or care if others want to read it. If you're participating in a class Book Club and your book isn't chosen by your classmates, you'll have to read a book that someone else brought in. Choose carefully!

For the actual Book Club Pitch, I ask my students to tell everyone what the book is about, why they want to read it, and where they found it. This takes a couple minutes, tops, and once everyone has pitched their book to the class we then form our book clubs based on the titles people want to read.

Once students have formed their book clubs, they meet in groups and take a bit of time to get to know each other. Then they set a reading schedule for their group and choose roles for the first book club meeting. And then comes the fun part, they read!

If you are forming a book club on your own, start a group email list so you can communicate with each other to figure out when and where you will meet, start reading, and enjoy!

READING FOR CLASS

Reading for Class
TEXTBOOKS AND CONTENT VOCABULARY

In the reading world we call this type of reading *content area* or *disciplinary reading*. The reading you will do for most of your classes will involve reading nonfiction texts such as textbooks, articles, word problems, charts, graphs, etc.

All of the reading skills we've discussed thus far will help you read *everything* you come across in life, whether it is for class or not. However, there are some special considerations to keep in mind when reading for class:

Textbooks

- If your teacher or professor does not activate your prior knowledge in class before you read a chapter in the book, **activate your own prior knowledge** before reading. This is the single most useful skill you have in your reading arsenal—use it!
- **Annotate** in your textbooks. If you don't want to write in the actual books themselves, buy some small Post-It notes and write on those, instead.
- **Create your own study guide** from the textbook using all of the information you identify as you go through your before, during, and after reading skills. Use your retellings to find gaps in your knowledge, and focus on those gaps in your study guides.
- Many modern textbooks are filled with extra **graphics** to help students make sense of the information included in them. Pay attention to these guides; they are there to help you.

- Similarly, textbooks often highlight or boldface **important terms** or **vocabulary words** for the content area—add these words to your juicy words list as soon as you come across them. Better yet—create a separate list for each content area class.
- Familiarize yourself with the organization of a chapter before you read it. This will help you anticipate what's coming next as you read.
- Similarly, flip to the end of a chapter before you read it and skim any summaries or chapter questions that are provided.

Content Vocabulary

- It is important that you **connect** the new words you learn in your content area classes to what you already know outside of that class. Remember—you only learn new information by connecting it to existing information, so doing this will help you learn these new words.
- If you have no existing knowledge with which to connect your new content vocabulary, **build your own prior knowledge**. You can do this by researching the subject on the Internet, building your own word knowledge for the words, or even flipping through your class textbook on your own.

Student Skills
THINK AND ACT LIKE A STUDENT

Student skills are all the skills and habits that help students perform their best. It's important to
develop your students skills because, without them, all of these reading skills you've just developed will go to waste.

What does a skilled student look like?

A skilled student looks like someone who **has it together**—you know the type I'm talking about:
he's on time to class, he remembers his homework and class materials, he's prepared for the exams, and he learns what he needs to learn.

In addition, a skilled student is focused—he has a purpose for being in school, and he is determined to achieve that purpose. (Sound familiar—*purpose*—get it?)

Student Skills In Class

Self-Advocate

Skilled students self-advocate. When you self-advocate, you actively pursue whatever you need to succeed in school. This could mean you contact your teacher or professor when you miss class, you make an appointment in your school's tutoring center when you need extra help, or you meet with your teacher or professor during her office hours to discuss a grade that you believe is unfair.

Whatever you do, when you self-advocate you take action in ensuring that you get everything you can get out of your education.

Build Relationships

Skilled students build relationships with their *instructors, classmates, advisors, tutors,* and any other people in the school with whom they interact. When you build a positive relationship with the people who make up your school community, you help ensure that you are going to get the most out of your time in school.

Building relationships with these people is as easy as *talking* to them. Find a study partner in your English class. Visit your teacher or professor during his office hours. Make an appointment with your advisor to discuss your academic plan. And then keep in touch. The more you feel connected to the school community, the better you'll do while you're there.

Another great way to build relationships on campus is to **get involved.** Join a club, or a sport, or a school group. Not only will you make great friends, you will become more connected to your school, and as a result you will likely perform better in your classes. Bonus!

Present Well

I'm sure you've heard the bromide, "you can't judge a book by its cover." Well, the truth is, presentation *does* count. Consider this: Would you take someone seriously if she wore a multi-colored mohawk wig to class? Probably not.

The way you behave in class, the way you either sit up or slump down in your chair, look alert or put your head down on your desk—all of these things affect others' perceptions of you. If your fellow classmates think you're a serious student, they're more likely to treat you as such. Same thing goes for your teachers and professors. And guess what? You will *feel* like a serious student if you start acting like one. (Ever heard the bromide: "Fake it till you make it"?)

Similarly, the way you present yourself *on paper* is also important. Don't submit work that is crumpled up, has tattered edges, or looks just plain sloppy. Rather, follow your teachers' or professors' guidelines for written work, and keep your papers flat and clean and organized in a binder or folder for class.

Student Skills Outside of Class

Preparation

By the time you arrive in class and take your seat, you should be well aware of what is going on that day and what the teacher or professor expects you to have done to prepare for the day's lesson. In order to be fully prepared:

- Keep an organized class binder with all of your class materials and work
  - When I was in college I bought a huge 3" binder and put ALL of my work for ALL of my classes in that one binder. I bought tab dividers to organize everything, and used this method for all four years of undergrad. This was great because I never forgot my work or brought the wrong work—it was all in one place!
- Keep the class syllabus in the front of your binder, and check it a day or two before each class to make sure you're on track
- Bring your binder and any textbooks or other materials to every class
- Bring a pen and a notebook or extra paper (this one seems obvious, but you'd be surprised how many students ask me if I have an extra pen.)
- Anticipate any conflicts in your schedule and meet with your instructors *before* they arrive to work out alternate arrangements
- Keep an agenda, and write any and all assignments, tests, readings, etc. in it.

- Join a study group! My college study group helped me get through all four years of classes, and we had some fun while we were at it, too. We met in the same place, every day, at the same time, and worked through everything together. And we ate a lot of snacks, which always helps.

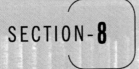

SECTION-**8**

BEFORE YOU GO

BEFORE YOU GO

Congratulations! You now know everything you need to know to improve your reading ability. In fact, at the end of every semester I tell my reading students that they know everything they need to know to *help others* improve their reading ability. Now you do, too.

The trick is to put all of this knowledge to use, and to turn these tips into ways of thinking in order to start getting more out of your reading. And that happens every time you pick something up to read. Be present. Be aware of how well you are (or aren't) focusing on the reading. Give yourself a break when you need one, and a push when that's more appropriate.

Be it a juicy vampire romance, or a classic piece of literature; an e-book read fifty words at a time on the tiny screen of an iPhone, or a golden-edged tome bound in an ornate leather cover; there are no *right* books to read, and there is no *right* way to read them. The only way you can go wrong is to not read anything at all.

It is my wish for you that you will discover the joy that comes from reading a good book. I have found endless entertainment, escape, revelation, delight, and companionship in books. And I hope you will, too.

Good luck, dear reader, and enjoy.

Acknowledgements

Thank you:

To my students, past, present, and future. It's a privilege.

To Ashley McDonald, for her editing expertise, and to Vasil Nazar, for his inspired design skills.

To David Stern and everyone at Eckhartz Press, a writer's publisher, truly.

To Mr. Dodd Mohr, my fifth grade teacher, who loved reading and teaching. I could tell.

To Ray Bradbury, for writing "A Sound of Thunder", and to Mr. Lloyd, for reading it with us in the seventh grade.

To Dr. Eric Twadell, who said, *You know you're going to be a teacher, right?*

To Dr. John Ahlgrim, who said, *Would you like to become a reading specialist?*

To Diane Covert, Gerry Daley, and Mary Winter, for giving me my first classrooms.

To Elpida Platis, Melissa Lindsey, Jennifer Staben, Amy Blumenthal, Olabisi Adenekan, and Deyanira Cardenas, for your friendship and collegiality, for believing in my Little Packet on Reading, and for making it better in the process.

To The Badass Book Club, you made my dream come true when you said yes.

To writers, who give us books to read, and readers, who give us reasons to write. And to you, may you discover the magic of it all.

And to my friends and family. Oh, you know why.